REYNAL'S WORLD HISTORY OF GREAT SCULPTURE

# GREAT SCULPTURE
# OF ANCIENT GREECE

REYNAL'S WORLD HISTORY OF GREAT SCULPTURE

# GREAT SCULPTURE
# OF ANCIENT GREECE

BY PIERRE DEVAMBEZ    Translated by Halina Tunikowska

REYNAL & COMPANY
in association with William Morrow & Company, Inc.
1978

*Here on the right:* Caryatid
*(detail) 420–406 B.C.; marble.*
*London, British Museum.*
*Originally located in the gallery*
*of Eretteo on the north side of the*
*Acropolis, the statue, along with others,*
*served as a supporting column.*

*On page 2:* The wedding of Hera and Zeus
*(detail), metope of temple E at Selinus,*
*about 460–450 B.C.; limestone and marble*
*with traces of color.*
*Palermo, National Museum*
*(see illustration page 129).*

*On page 6:* Head of a Woman,
*Cretan art XIII century B.C.; painted limestone.*
*Athens, National Archeological Museum.*
*An example of pre-Greek art from Mycenae,*
*the head probably had a religious function.*

## REYNAL'S WORLD HISTORY OF GREAT SCULPTURE

Editorial Director
LORENZO CAMUSSO
Scientific Consultant
MIA CINOTTI

## GREAT SCULPTURE OF ANCIENT GREECE

Text
PIERRE DEVAMBEZ
Translated by
HALINA TUNIKOWSKA
List of works
GEMMA VERCHI
Notes
ANNA CARPI
Picture research
NICOLETTA POLTRI TANUCCI
Layout
GIOVANNI MELADA
Editorial assistant
MICHELE BUZZI
Editorial secretary
ADA JORIO

Translation copyright © 1978 by Arnoldo Mondadori Editore, Milano
First published in the United States by Reynal and Company, Inc.
Originally published in Italian in 1978 by Arnoldo Mondadori
Editore, Milano under the title GRECIA
Copyright © 1978 by Mondadori-Shogakukan
Photograph copyright © 1978 by Shogakukan Ltd., Tokyo, Japan
Text copyright © 1978 by Mondadori-Shogakukan
Library of Congress Catalog Card Number 78-55511
ISBN 0-688-61203-3
Printed and bound in Italy by Officine Grafiche di Arnoldo
Mondadori Editore, Verona

CONTENTS

# IMAGES
# OF BEAUTY

**As the bottom of the sea lies peaceful
beneath a foaming surface,
a great soul lies sedate beneath the strife
of passions in Greek figures.**

(Johann Joachim Winckelmann, *Gedanken
über die Nachahmung der griechischen Werke
in der Malerei und Bildhauerkunst*, 1755.
English translation, Henry Fuseli,
*Reflections on the Painting and Sculpture of
the Greeks*, London, 1765.

## The Archaic Period
## From the Eighth Century to 480 B.C.

We regard sculpture as the most important of the Greek arts, the art of ancient Greece *par excellence*. Free-standing and relief sculpture played a more important part in the life of that period than it does today, and in Greek sculpture we find one of the most perfect and complete expressions of Hellenism.

Contrary to what was once thought, sculpture emerged slowly and cautiously, but because it was such an essential part of Greek life artists had to try to solve the technical problems they encountered in order to satisfy their increasingly demanding customers. Sculpture was a necessity to the Greeks, and so, although throughout the course of its development Greek artists always did their best to produce works that were "beautiful to look at" (to echo the phrase proudly carved on one of the earliest examples), beauty was not their main preoccupation. It was not from a pure love of art that the Greeks commissioned their artists to produce the reliefs and statues that are now regarded as museum pieces. In fact, except at the very end of the age of Greek colonial supremacy, both free-standing and relief sculpture had a specific function, one that was always connected with religious beliefs or the practices of a cult.

This is very apparent in the early examples, which by the eighth century can be regarded as genuinely Hellenic. These were small figurines—about 12 centimeters (4.5 inches) high, but sometimes much less—made of terra cotta, bronze, precious metals, alabaster and even ivory, and they have been found in graves or buried under sanctuaries. Responding to the primitive, magic idea that an image was actually the same thing as the being it portrayed, artists made figures of protect-ing deities to watch over the people who had dedicated them or over the dead they were buried with. Also found have been figures of cattle, horses, and mares suckling their foals (it was thought the sight of a mothering animal would persuade the gods to guarantee fertility). There are also many examples of similar votive offerings dedicated in sanctuaries that were made in Greece and elsewhere during the Bronze Age and during the transitional period leading to the Iron Age.

But what was new was the Greeks' way of seeing reality. Modern critics have called the art of pre-Hellenic civilizations "impressionist," in close touch with nature, spontaneous, interested in the most vivid stance, and unconcerned with detail the eye could not take in at first glance. All these were features that had been forgotten to such a great extent at the beginning of the eighth century that the figurines that were produced immediately prior to that seem crude and completely lacking in style. But once the tribes which had for generations been migrating into Greece from the north gained a strong foothold and became totally integrated with the indigenous population, an entirely new and genuinely Hellenic character emerged.

The recording of visual impressions, which, though true to life, were superficial and transitory, was replaced by an intellectual approach that tried to produce an archetype of the object being portrayed by taking its structure apart. Like children attempting to draw for the first time, the Greeks portrayed the subject not so much by looking at it as by remembering what they knew about it. In a sense, they reconstituted it. It was therefore the structure that the Greeks emphasized, though their lack of technical skill may perhaps have pushed them towards caricature. Their aim was to make the most typical features stand out as clearly as possible.

The horse's nobility and speed set it apart from

other species, so the Greek sculptor perched it on very long legs with well-designated joints, set its head proudly on a well-arched chest, and gave it a long tail that reached down to the ground. And it did not matter if the barrel of the body was only a small cylinder squashed between the front and hind quarters, since a rider's pride was not involved. A man is a creature of strength and suppleness, so the sculptor exaggerated the breadth of his shoulders, emphasized the curve of the hips separating the top half of the body from the bottom, made his legs—which were used for running—much longer, and elongated the neck. Obviously all this made for a certain amount of stiffness, and the desire to split up the figure into its constituent elements sometimes gave it a disjointed appearance.

When Polyclitus produced his *Doryphorus* three centuries later in *c.* 450–440 B.C., drawing on his abilities and the experience gained by his predecessors, but at the same time correcting by direct observation any abstract tendencies his work may have had, he was responding to the same wish to portray not a specific individual but a perfect archetypal athlete.

This rigidity is therefore one of the fundamental characteristics of Hellenic sculpture and of Hellenic art in general. It is unusual that the examples we have just given come from mainland Greece and especially from the Peloponnesus, for it was there that the Doric spirit was particularly dominant. Although the Ancient Greeks had not been completely cut off from each other and there had been frequent communication and trade among them, they attached a historical or, more accurately, a genealogical importance to whether they were descended from the Dorians or their cousins the Ionians (who took their name from their ancestor Ionis). The Dorians, who were laconic, determined, and proud of the fact that their strength made them the best athletes, had spread from mainland Greece (which was nevertheless always to remain their spiritual home) on to the island of Crete and particularly into southern Italy and Sicily. Their ideal of art was virile. But the second group, who had settled in Attica, on the Aegean islands and the western coast of Asia Minor, were easygoing and loved listening to long rambling tales—the poems of Homer, for example—during their lavish meals. Constant contact with their rich Oriental neighbours had given them a taste for finery, luxury, and ornament. The jewelry found in the graves of rich Athenians—small metal plates and embossed gold fillets portraying Asiatic-type goddesses flanked by sacred animals or lines of warriors or deer—is Oriental in inspiration and construction.

Nevertheless it would be wrong to suggest that these foreign countries influenced no one but the Ionians and then only their minor arts. The emergence of large-scale sculpture in Greece coincided with the growth of maritime communications, and, from the middle of the seventh century, there appeared in various parts of the Hellenic world—in Crete, on the Aegean islands bordering Anatolia, and in Attica (places that were the most open to foreign influence)—statues based on models from Syria, Cyprus, and especially Egypt. The statues were life-size, sometimes larger, and the reason for this was the logical necessity of making sure the faithful could see the deities that Homer had described so vividly, so like the human beings they ruled over, standing behind the sacrificial altars of the temples that had recently been built to house them.

These statues were not simply enlargements of earlier figurines, which would in any case have been difficult to produce. They were conceived differently and were undoubtedly copies of Egyptian statues standing on the banks of the Nile. Their stance—hieratic, upright, feet flat on the ground, left foot slightly advanced, head straight and facing the front—was as suited to portraying the immortals worshiped by crowds of people as it was to depicting the faithful who wanted to erect a stone or bronze statue of themselves in a sanctuary, or the dead rising from the grave to make sure their burial rites were being carried out. Apart from an occasional inscription, a characteristic attribute, or the fact that the statue came from a cemetery, there is nothing that now enables us to tell whether it portrayed someone who had died, a devout mortal, or a deity. And that is why we use generic terms to describe them: *kouroi* (singular, *kouros*) for the men and *korai* (singular, *kore*) for the young women. Artists deliberately chose to make both *kouroi* and *korai* young and did nothing to make them look like any particular individual. They were the formalized embodiment of an ideal type. The young men were shown naked, like strapping godlike athletes (pp. 42, 96–98), while the women were decked out with jewelry and dressed in their most beautiful clothes. A love of finery that was imperative in the ritual context of religion was also evident in the care reserved for the hairstyle (the same for both women and men): a long mane covering the back and falling in tresses down to the upper part of the chest (pp. 43, 117).

The unrealistic colours in which the figures were painted (red eyes and lips, blue hair, and multi-coloured garments) gave them a slightly barbaric appearance. Except in the case of a few *korai*, generally the oldest, who have the lower part of their bodies sheathed in floor-length dresses that form a solid base, all these figures have one foot placed in front of the other, which gives them a certain amount of stability. The fact that this leg is always the left one shows how closely Greek artists kept to Egyptian models (according to Greek superstition the left side was unlucky).

Movement is what is lacking most in this series of *kouroi* and *korai*, which throughout the sixth century formed the bulk of sculptural output in all parts of Greece. The religious climate may have required the frontal stance, but it was for technical reasons that the arms remained joined to the body for such a long time, pressed against the chest or thighs: artists were afraid the limbs would break at the join or at the elbow. Slowly and tentatively, however, they were bent forward in a gesture of prayer or offering.

Perhaps it was when these bronze statues became generally more lifelike and their limbs lost their customary rigidity that sculpture gained a new impetus. The homogeneity and ductility of bronze make it stronger than stone, which always tends to break in the weak spots; another point to remember is that the clay of the preparatory maquettes was very easy to work. As soon as the Greeks learned how to join the separately made pieces with solder (before the middle of the sixth century) bronze statues became very popular, even more so than marble ones, but we know very little about them since most were melted down when bronze became scarce and had to be salvaged for practical needs (the manufacture of arms and money). Sharp tools were used to carve the stone, marble, and soft poros limestone (apparently the same method was used to carve the early wooden statues—xoana, xoanon in the singular). This produced planes separated by sharp edges that had to be smoothed down to connect the various surfaces, and it is for this reason that details on the oldest works made of stone, particularly details of musculature, were engraved with a point. The more malleable clay used for the maquettes, however, was better suited to creating volume, and the transition from convex to concave was made imperceptibly.

Yet mastering materials and tools was hardly enough. To give the impression, the illusion, of life, which was always the aim of Greek art, sculptors had to first become familiar with the complex structure of the human body. The inflexibility of the *kouros* and *kore* types had precluded all creative initiative and forced sculptors to concentrate on portraying anatomy and drapery. Using foreign models as well as their inherent sense of "harmonious proportion," they had from the outset constructed the human body according to natural proportions and worked out the normal relationships between its various parts. And this also applied to the enormous statues, which could reach a height of some 10 meters (32 feet) or more, that were sometimes produced, particularly around 600 B.C.

The structure of each of these parts of the body and the intricacy of the drapery posed the hardest problem. We cannot at this stage go into the sculptors' dogged and systematic attempts to work this out, nor show how they finally succeeded, at first concentrating on the smallest details before hitting upon the idea of coordinating them into a coherent whole. The main thing to remember is that, far from aiming for a particular likeness, they always tried to turn the statue they were making into an ideal: the flawless body of a perfect athlete or an invariably beautiful woman. The expressions on the faces of the statues are also impersonal, and the smile that appeared on their lips in the second half of the sixth century was only the reflection of an inner life an artist had no other way of showing, but without which the statue might look as if it had no soul. The differences between these perfect figures, which are all young and eager to please, all made for the same purpose according to predetermined types, do not lie in the individuality of the subjects but in the sculptor's style. Or rather in the style of the school or workshop to which he belonged—because in these formative years it is difficult to judge the individual characteristics of artists trying to master technical problems.

To identify the schools and differentiate among them we must look beyond the *kouroi* and *korai*, for although they were the most often depicted types in the Archaic period, they were not the only kind of sculpture that was produced in the seventh and sixth centuries. Among the Greeks who commissioned votive statues of themselves there were those who wanted to spell out the meaning of what they were doing and the occasion of their dedication. There is the Attic statue of the *Moschophorus* for example (p. 41), which dates from about the middle of the sixth century (the figure has a sacrificial calf slung over his shoulders, and his name means "calf bearer" in Greek); or there is the slightly later statue of an elegant nobleman sitting proudly on the horse that has won a race for him (*Rampin Horseman*, p. 107). Both these life-size marble sculptures are singular examples of a genre more commonly made on a smaller scale as bronze figurines. The hieratic immobility of figures that were previously frozen in dignified or deferential attitudes is replaced by movement dictated by action, movement that shatters certain conventions such as the "law of frontality": the *Rampin Horseman* is clearly turning his head towards a cheering crowd.

Nevertheless, free-standing sculpture is not as well suited as relief to portraying either groups of people or narrative and action, and the two closely entwined bronze statuettes from the middle of the sixth century (now thought to depict Zeus wrestling with Typhon and not a man fighting with a centaur) are quite exceptional. In fact, this period saw various parts of the Greek world producing a great many mythological reliefs containing more than one figure. The scenes were embossed or cut in metal votive discs, cuirasses, sword-belt and shoulder-belt plates, and tripod supports; or they were impressed on the neck and body of large terracotta jars or carved on wooden or ivory panels.

These small or medium-sized artifacts were almost always produced for the sheer amusement of the people who bought them, and they demonstrate a taste for narrative coupled with a feeling for composition that was to be developed still more in monumental relief when, in the first quarter of the sixth century, buildings intended for religious worship became larger and required figurative decoration.

The problem the artist was then faced with was no longer how to balance and stabilize his figures as in free-standing sculpture, but how to design his composition and adapt it to a framework that was dictated by a building's architecture. The most visible spot on a temple or similar monument was obviously the pediment dominating the two façades, but its triangular shape was also the most difficult to fill, since the height of the figures had to decrease steadily from the middle to the two corners. That was why in the earliest periods (in Corfu for example) either the unity of the composition would be broken by juxtaposing several themes, each treated on a different scale, or by putting several tightly coiled serpentine figures at the ends of the two wings. Only at the end of the Archaic period (in Aegina) did artists hit upon the idea of showing a battle scene by starting from the middle and having the soldiers first standing upright, then leaning forward to attack, finally sprawling dead or wounded on the ground (pp. 46, 122–23, 125). The square or rectangular framework of the Doric metope forced the artist to use restraint. Knowing that he would very likely destroy the unity of his composition by dividing it into several panels separated by the vertical grooving of the triglyphs (as happened in the Sicyonian Treasury at Delphi), the artist had to cut it down to basics and give it dramatic character by using a very small number of figures.

The votive or funerary stele made for a sanctuary or cemetery was also narrow, but it was wide enough to carry a figure of the deceased rising out of the next world, or of the votary who had dedicated it standing in front of his deity. It was in fact simply a cheaper method of representation, but its function was the same as that of the free-standing sculptures we have already discussed, and it was not until the fifth century that scenes were depicted on these small monuments. Only with the continuous Ionic frieze were sculptors able to let themselves go, even though there was a great danger that this freedom might lead to repetitive and overelaborate decoration.

Like free-standing sculpture, relief sculpture was also linked to religion, but, whereas the former was concerned with recording a cult act, the function of relief (discounting votive and funerary scenes) was to decorate the temple and its outbuildings, for example the treasuries that were built in international sanctuaries to house the gifts the city had received. It was undoubtedly decoration, but it was never secular. At the beginning its role was sometimes apotropaic (to ward off evil), and indeed the Gorgons in the middle of the Corfu pediments, or the Gorgon carved on a cornerstone at Didyma, were there to protect the building against evil influence. But its aim was sometimes to glorify gods and heroes by depicting their achievements. Greek reliefs contain none of the ordinary scenes common in our cathedrals; the work stays within the holy precincts of mythology. Discounting major themes, mythological scenes often involve local legend. Though the adventures of Heracles (Latin Hercules) and Theseus were popular throughout the Hellenic world, other episodes, particularly in Sicily and southern Italy, refer to such specific traditions that we now find them difficult to understand. Other events that were commemorated were the victories the gods had helped the Greeks to win over the centaurs and Trojans (and this indicates to what extent fact and fable were intertwined at this period). It was only towards the end of the sixth century, at Delphi, that the work dominating the main façade of the temple stopped telling a simple story and became instructive.

By examining the style and characteristics of all these genres of sculpture (statuary, small-scale sculpture, and relief) archaeologists have tried to find out where the main workshops were located. There were many of them, and in those days of ready mobility there was frequent contact between them. In fact, when the Spartans, who in any case had their share of artists, wanted to decorate the sanctuary of Apollo at Amyclae, they arranged for a sculptor to come from Ionian Magnesia, and this kind of interchange produced considerable similarities between the earliest *korai*, whether they were from Crete (*Auxerre Goddess*, p. 92), the Cyclades (*Nikandra of Delos*, p. 91), or from Claros in Asia Minor.

There was great activity everywhere. Outside Crete, where there is a fine continuous frieze on a small religious monument at Prinia, the main Doric centers were all in the Peloponnesus. The sculptor of the two *kouroi* known as *Cleobis and Biton* (p. 96), dedicated at Delphi at the very beginning of the sixth century, was from Argos. And although this area's large-scale sculpture has now disappeared, local craftsmen have been credited with a great many well-made bronze statuettes that used to have round mirrors placed on their head and raised arms.

Corinthian figurines were made for the same purpose, but they were more delicate. Corinth had built its prosperity on commerce and played an important part in the history of Archaic sculpture. The *Tenea Apollo* (p. 97), a *kouros* which dates from about 550 B.C., may seem a bit lifeless, but his slender proportions, smooth contours, and the beginnings of a smile on his face give him a grace that sets him apart from his Doric brothers.

Gorgon, *from the Corfu temple pediment, Archaic art*, c. 575 B.C. *Corfu, Archeological Museum.*

Another example of Corinthian art is the oldest pediment known to us (*c.* 575 B.C., mentioned above and illustrated on p. 13). It was made in the Corinthian colony of Kerkira (Corfu) and portrays a huge Gorgon flanked by two panthers, on either side of which are two smaller-scale figures: on one side a seated goddess and, on the other, Zeus angrily smiting a giant with a thunderbolt.

Still in the northern Peloponnesus, we come to the small city of Sicyon. The only works that can be ascribed with any certainty to its famous school of sculpture are the metopes of the small treasury that was dedicated at Delphi just before the middle of the sixth century. They are powerful works, even savage, but extraordinarily lifelike; for example, the scene showing huntsmen chasing a wild Calydonian boar. The technique is advanced, and, for the first time in relief, the figures are shown *en face*.

We ought also to mention Sparta, which had not yet withdrawn into its magnificent and unproductive isolation, since, apart from its many agile figurines, it was undoubtedly this school that produced the huge head of Hera (*c.* 600 B.C.), the only one that has survived out of a group of deities at Olympia (p. 108).

The prolific output of Sicily and Magna Graecia was also Doric, although influenced by the art of eastern Greece. The metopes of Temple C at Selinus, those at Paestum, and those on religious buildings (perhaps treasuries) in the neighbouring site of Silarus (Foce del Sele) illustrate legends that do not always appear to have been known elsewhere, and the striking thing about them is their boldness and their sense of the picturesque and the dramatic, unparalleled in the rest of the Hellenic world.

Even though we still do not have enough information about Asia Minor, we do know that sculpture was also produced on a large and varied scale in Ionia. Some works, from areas on the edge of the continent, betray the influence of neighbouring Levantine civilizations, for example the Milesian statues of weighty dignitaries sitting or rather slumped in easy chairs. But farther west, in the islands, the feeling was more subtle. The faces of statues from Samos exude intelligence; the Hera dedicated by Cheramyes (p. 95), one of many similar ones, is also from Samos. It is a magnificently statuesque body, full of life in spite of the stylization of contour and drapery.

There were workshops on a number of Aegean islands: Naxos was for a long time the most prolific. Towards the beginning of the sixth century, enormous *kouroi*, which were not always finished, were carved from the local coarse-grained marble, as were, on a smaller scale, strange, sharp-featured figures and the thin lionesses the inhabitants of Delos lined up in the Oriental manner along a terrace facing the Sacred Lake. The schools of Paros, Chios, and others it is now difficult to identify were less severe. The *kouroi* are not as sturdy and accurate as those from the Doric world, and the *korai* are particularly coquettish. Typically Ionic are the friezes the inhabitants of Siphnos commissioned Cycladic artists to make for their treasury at Delphi in about 525 B.C.: battling gods and giants, and fighting Greeks and Trojans watched by the assembled Olympians (pp. 44–45, 98–99, 100, 101). The scenes, covering the entire length of the continuous frieze, are full of life and picturesque detail reminiscent of Homer's tales. Everything was painted in the customary bright colours, and there are inscriptions to identify the characters. This carefree exuberance would undoubtedly have formed a really striking contrast next to the slightly arid terseness of the Doric metopes on the Sicyonian Treasury.

Attic sculpture is usually placed between these two tendencies, and we can follow the systematic development of its monumental art from the unsophisticated pediments decorating small buildings on the Acropolis in the first quarter of the sixth century (showing Heracles being admitted to Olympus or fighting with the Hydra or being watched by a benevolent three-headed monster as he struggles with a snake, to the skillful decoration on the treasury built in Delphi immediately after the Marathon victory. The composition was clumsy at first, but gradually adapted to the framework. The pediments of two temples, the Hekatompedon on the Acropolis and the Delphi temple decorated by the Athenian Antenor, enable us to estimate their date at about 520 B.C. Although the design is still rather uncoordinated in these works, spiritual cohesion has already been achieved.

Particularly fine in the first is the tight grouping of Athena and Enceladus, showing the goddess leaning forward (following the slope of the roof) to wound the giant, who has half fallen to the ground.

The magnificence of this subject, which was chosen to pay tribute to the power of the immortals, is very far removed from the charming but inconsequential inspiration of previous periods. The unifying element behind the huge composition, linking all the characters who are taking part in what is going on singly or in pairs, is religious inspiration. The same can be said about the Delphi temple. The main façade does not depict some brave exploit but the figure of Apollo himself, an even more impressive subject designed to uplift the faithful standing in front of the temple, and though the various figures are separate they are united in their devout introspection. Unity of inspiration is one of the main achievements of Athenian sculpture, and, however different their internal composition might be, the metopes on each side of the Delphi treasury are devoted to a single theme—the Amazonomachy, the exploits of Heracles and Theseus—and the same feeling runs through all of them, the same wish to commemorate the triumph of Hellenism.

This wish to express the physical aspect of life as well as its moral depth can be clearly seen in the long series of *kouroi* and *korai* that have been excavated on the Acropolis, in Athenian sanctuaries and cemeteries, and in the surrounding areas. They were influenced by other schools for a very long time, those of Ionia in particular, but they are more delicate and at the same time more stately. However, as soon as tyranny gave way to democratic rule between 520 and 510 B.C., and increasingly when the Persians threatened to invade the country at the beginning of the fifth century, sobriety took over and the figures seem to be weighed down by the burden of a new responsibility. The *Blond Boy* and the *Euthydicus Kore* (known as the *Pouting Kore*), actually produced during the Persian wars, no longer have the pleasant smile of previous periods. They look almost sad, or in any event lost in thought.

It was when the Greeks finally beat back the invaders in 480 B.C. that the Archaic period finally came to an end. The formative years were followed by a serious adolescence that already contained something of the maturity of the Age of Pericles. The temple on the island of Aegina, which had been built during the transition from one period to the next, is characteristic of this crucial epoch. Several years separate the carving of the two pediments. They both depict fighting Greeks and Trojans, and in both there are symmetrically grouped pairs of warriors on each side of the tall figure of Athena. But on the west pediment, which illustrates the war described by Homer, the figures are stiffer and have more obviously been influenced by the island's famous bronze casters. In addition, they have been more clumsily arranged, and the recumbent figures in the two corners face outwards. The east pediment is devoted to an earlier war in which Heracles had participated (pp. 46, 122–23, 125). It is more balanced and centered more clearly; it is also more lively, and the goddess, no longer motionless, appears to be taking part in the battle. Nothing then stood in the way of rapid progress. The next period, which was to last until about 450 B.C., is called "pre-Classical."

## Pre-Classicism

The thirty years or so that separate the battles of Salamis (480 B.C.) and Plataea (479 B.C.) from the time peace was finally made with Persia represent a period of extraordinarily productive ferment for the whole of Greece. The unexpected victories that had enabled the Greeks to drive Xerxes' huge army out of Greek territory and their victory at Himera, which had saved Sicily from invasion by Carthage, gave them boundless faith in their own strength as well as infinite gratitude to the gods who had made these triumphs possible.

These successes coincided with the time when sculptors finally solved all the technical problems that had for so long been hampering their efforts to produce really lifelike works. The Acropolis *Critian Boy*, which was probably carved just before 480 B.C., differs from his *kouroi* predecessors in the freedom of his stance. The old law of frontality has been abandoned, the overrigid symmetry has been broken, and the weight of the body is no longer equally distributed on the two legs, which means that the shoulders and hips no longer lie horizontal. The head is slightly lowered and inclined towards the right. The anatomy has been more closely observed; it is more as it appears in real life. The lines of the groin may form too sharp a dividing line between the thighs and torso, but the latter is carved

delicately and smoothly, coordinating elements that were once disjointed and separate into a harmonious and coherent whole. This achievement of organic unity after such a long period of experiment marked the beginning of Classicism in Greek sculpture.

From now on there was a new element in sculpture, even when it was no longer a question of an individual piece but a group, as for example the *Harmodius and Aristogiton* group that was made in 477 B.C. by Critius (who is also thought to have carved the *Critian Boy*) with the help of the bronze caster Nesiotes. The two heroes, who were regarded as the saviours of Athens (although they ultimately failed), stand side by side in reversed symmetry. They each have a distinct personality, but it is only the presence of the other figure that brings this out to its full extent. The unifying element behind the two figures is their joint action and their shared feelings.

Although there are other works proving the excellence of Athenian sculpture during this period, this city was not the only place where it was being produced. Of the many examples scattered throughout the Greek world, those in southern Italy and Sicily were the most brilliant. The metopes of Temple E at Selinus may portray the impressive *Marriage of Zeus and Hera* (though it has been suggested the figures could be Dionysius and Persephone), but the picturesque and realistic side has not been overlooked, as, for example, the scene with Heracles and the Amazon. Locri produced small votive plaques (*pinakes*) that are just as important from the artistic point of view as they are to the history of religion. The stately and slightly frigid goddess now in the Berlin Museum was undoubtedly carved out of Locri marble, as possibly were the three large panels known as the *Ludovisi Throne* or *Triptych* (pp. 55, 56, 120), although what they were intended for and what

16

they mean remains a mystery. The panel that has been worked out best shows a young woman, dressed in a sheer tunic, rising above a veil held up by two maidservants leaning over her—Hera's prenuptial bath or Aphrodite emerging from the sea? The second interpretation is probably closer to the mark, since the two side panels illustrate two aspects of love: a completely naked girl playing a flute, and a married woman, modestly wrapped in a peplos and ritually burning incense. The work is fresh, full of intense religious feeling, and the workmanship is meticulous, firm and delicate at the same time.

We find the same precision and majestic simplicity in one of the very rare original bronzes that has survived: the *Delphi Charioteer* (pp. 53, 119). The standing figure is dressed in his uniform of ankle-length, high-waisted tunic and is still holding the horses' reins in his hands. He was originally shown in a chariot, next to his master Polyzalos, the tyrant of Gela, who was thus commemorating the victory of his quadriga at the Delphi games. Unfortunately the figure of Polyzalos has disappeared, as have the horses and the chariot itself. Although he has slightly turned his head and shoulders towards the crowd, the charioteer knows the cheering is directed at the prince, and he stands aside modestly. His face has the shy seriousness of youth, and the slenderness of his build is emphasized by the long, straight folds furrowing his tunic from the waist down, like the fluting of a column. Yet there is nothing motionless about the figure. Even though he is standing still, we are conscious of his energy, quivering with suppressed life just beneath the surface; and the strength of his arms is emphasized, but not overstated, by the firmness and accuracy with which the artist has depicted the veins and tendons.

It is because of this last feature (but equally because the winner was Sicilian) that scholars have tentatively attributed this masterpiece to the bronze caster Pythagoras, a native of Samos who later settled in Rhegium on the strait of Messina. Pythagoras was well known for the meticulous way he portrayed veins and tendons. However, he was valued most for his ability to portray movement, not the potential movement of a figure that clearly has the capacity to spring into life even though it is not moving, nor even movement that has been stopped (as in the large bronze found in the open sea off Euboea, which, legs apart and one arm outstretched, is flourishing a weapon in the other— (a thunderbolt or a trident, thus identifying the figure as either Zeus or Poseidon), but movement arrested in midstream as if by a snapshot. Pythagoras, a predecessor and possibly a rival of Myron, produced numerous statues of athletes, showing them at the most crucial moment of the sport in which they excelled. They were always in disequilibrium, but his ability to make them appear balanced amazed his contemporaries.

It is in the Peloponnesus that we find the most important monumental building of this period. Between 470 and 456 B.C. a large temple in honour of Zeus was built at Olympia. Its carved decoration consists of twelve metopes in high relief, arranged in groups of six on the façades and pediments; the figures are free-standing and detached from the background, as they are at Aegina, Delphi, and the Hekatompedon. The west pediment, dominated by the tall figure of Apollo the judge (p. 127), illustrates Lapiths and centaurs fighting savagely (pp. 50, 124, 126). The other pediment, looking deceptively peaceful, portrays the dramatic start of the chariot race that was to make the hero Pelops lord of the Peloponnesus as well as the husband of Hippodamia. Her father, Oenomaus, who has until then governed the area, has been told by an oracle that his daughter's husband will kill him and take his place, so he has already eliminated several suitors by putting a condition on the marriage: that Hippodamia's hand will belong to whoever can beat him in a chariot race. Thanks to his fast horses he has always managed to come in first and has subsequently killed his opponents. But, protected by the gods, who have become tired of Oenomaus' crimes, Pelops wins the race when an accident causes the tyrannical king's death. It would have been difficult to show the course or outcome of the race within the restricted space of a pediment: the agony of the main characters and their friends just before the start of the race was much more moving. The only ones who know in advance what will happen are the two thoughtful soothsayers in the background and Zeus himself, standing along the axis of the composition. Certainly no Greek was unfamiliar with this legend: it commemorated the inauguration of the most important competition in the Olympic Games, as well as the justice of the immortals. But the atmosphere of the scene was such that the suspense must have been real. The figures are simply arranged side by side and do not touch. The main thing that gives the work its unity is the anxiety shared by its component figures, from those outstretched in the corners (the personifications of two neighbouring rivers, Cladeus and Alpheus), glancing curiously towards the middle, to the two groups around Zeus: on the left the villains Oenomaus and his wife Sterope, and on the right, in the place of honour, Pelops and Hippodamia. Even the apparently neutral figures of a boy and girl (slave and maidservant) standing behind the poised chariots in the two wings of the pediment, following the slope of the roof, participate in the general emotion.

The west pediment, on the other hand, is full of tumultuous, unremitting movement. Only the central figure of Apollo stands detached, his right arm raised in a gesture of peace. The groups of fighters form an arabesque of linked figures. Yet the violence seems controlled: a centaur seizes a woman, who tries to escape by wrenching her body around and pushing against him with the back of her arm; a Lapith is almost sprawled out on the ground, bracing himself on one knee to push his opponent back; a monster bites his adversary to escape from his grip—all this clearly demonstrates how fierce the fighting is. But the battle unfolds rhythmically, and this is what gives the work harmonious cohesion. We do not know what the exact composition of the pediment was because it was found in pieces, but, whatever it may originally have looked like, what stands out is the artist's concern that the spectator's eye should move along the work without being halted by any obstacles. The faces of the centaurs are contorted in pain or anger, but their opponents—the representatives of civilization—know how to control their feelings, and even the women, who are in the most danger, remain calm. Theseus' face is even more impassive and remote, although his violent gesture suggests that he is upset to see that the banquet, to which the king of the Lapiths has invited him to celebrate his daughter's marriage, has degenerated into a brawl.

Love of contrast is by itself not enough to explain the differences between the two pediments. Both are inspired by religion, but the events they portray are not of the same significance. The Centauromachy is just a popular episode, almost an anecdote, and Apollo does not have much trouble calming the drunken guests. But the setting up of the Olympic Games and the founding of a Peloponnesian dynasty that was to number many famous figures among its descendants were historically much more important to the Greeks; the lord of Olympus had to intervene in person.

It is in this pediment that the Doric character is most apparent, which is only to be expected in the chief sanctuary of the Peloponnesus. The figures are not distorted by any violent movement but are shown at their sturdiest, at their closest to the ideal of moderation that typified the art of Argos and other large cities in the Peloponnesus; the statues could be said to possess an architectural stateliness. The name of the sculptor who produced these magnificent pieces is unknown.

The Centauromachy was conceived and produced by another artist, also unknown. In spite of its savagery, there is a degree of softness in the relief which seems to contain traces of Ionic influence. The metopes have survived patchily; some are almost intact, others are badly damaged. Each one is devoted to one of the labours of Heracles; the hero's patroness (the goddess Athena) is shown by his side in most of them. The small number of figures was well suited to the framework in which the artist had to work, and the composition in each is admirably varied. Heracles displays all his strength when he catches the Cretan bull—his muscles swell and his feet strain against the ground. But when he gives the goddess the birds he has caught beside Lake Stymphalus he looks calm and quiet, heartened by the welcome he gets from his patroness, who was said to have the artlessness of a country shepherd girl. However, the most moving metope (unfortunately badly damaged) is the one in which the hero, after his first victory (over the Nemean Lion), appears weighed down by the prospect of the many ordeals he will yet have to tackle for the good of mankind.

Certain characteristics, for instance the fact that it does not attempt to exhaust a subject but leaves various possibilities open, indicate that the art of the period we have just examined is not yet entirely Classical. It has a youthful freshness with all the boundless opportunities of maturity before it; it has solved all its teething problems but does not yet have the self-confidence of adulthood. Artists feel they still have much to accomplish. The Classic ideal was not to be achieved until some years later, with the beginning of the Age of Pericles. The period was brief, but it was a time that saw the crystallization of what two or three generations before had been regarded as the quintessence of Hellenism.

## Fifth-Century Classicism

The Early Classical period actually amounts to less than fifty years, from the end of the war against Persia and other wars in which Greek cities fought each other (448–447 B.C.), to the fall of Athens, conquered in 404 B.C. by its old rival Sparta. But it was during this short span that three of antiquity's greatest sculptors, all very different from each other, were active, together with many others who were less famous.

The bronze caster Myron came from the rugged mountain area lying between Attica and Boeotia. He is often regarded as an innovator, but what he actually did was to carry through trends that had appeared in vase paintings during the last phase of the Archaic period at the end of the sixth century and the beginning of the fifth. Like Pythagoras, he wanted to capture the most extreme movement at its moment of unsteady equilibrium. His work—like that of his contemporaries and the majority of sculptors in the round who were active until the end of antiquity—has been lost, and we have nothing to go on but the copies and replicas (some good, others less so) by means of which archeologists try to reconstruct the appearance of the originals. Myron's most famous work is the *Discobolus* (p. 183). Knees bent, body leaning forward, the athlete is brandishing in his outstretched right hand the heavy bronze discus he is about to throw. His coiled body quivers all over and its intensity is so great that we overlook the impossibility of his stance; it is too fleeting for the eye to grasp. The angle the statue is supposed to be viewed from is indicated by the position of the legs, shown in profile, as is the right side with its highlighted ribs. But the abdomen, pivoting sharply on the hips, is shown in three-quarter view, the shoulders are almost frontal, while the head, slightly lowered, is turned towards the left. A daring combination that had its roots in Archaism, but Myron was expert enough to make it look apparently natural, thanks to the energy of the whole figure. It is this energy that holds our gaze, as well as the strength of the musculature, which is powerful without being overstated. There is a strong contrast between the smooth surface of the chest and the very marked relief of the stomach, the sinewy limbs and the delicate way the artist has depicted the fingers. But the face remains impassive and the features are not in any way distorted by the athlete's exertion.

The original of the bronze cow that the ancient Greeks regarded as one of Myron's masterpieces has not survived, but we have copies of a two-figure group that was dedicated on the Acropolis. The figures in this group are ranged side by side, to be viewed in profile as if in a bas-relief. They portray the satyr Marsyas dancing forward on tiptoe to try to seize a flute Athena has just contemptuously thrown down. The goddess moves away slowly, but Marsyas has been represented in the act of starting back with his body arched and his legs bent.

Polyclitus of Argos also used bronze, but his work is completely different. A few years younger than Myron—who was at the height of his fame just after 440 B.C.—Polyclitus came from Sicyon in the Peloponnesus. His work had many Doric tendencies, and its lack of variety was thought surprising by his contemporaries. His output was small, and although he produced a chryselephantine statue of Hera for her sanctuary (the Heraion) at Argos, his adopted country, his main subjects were athletes. His athletes were not shown in the heat of action, as Myron's athletes were, but standing at ease (like the *kouroi* of the Archaic period) so as to display the beauty of the human body at its best. Polyclitus wanted to portray the perfect, harmonious human body. And many artists of the succeeding generations took his figures as their models.

The athletes appear to have been sculpted to illustrate his book (now unfortunately lost), entitled the *Kanon* ("Rule"), in which he laid down what he considered the perfect proportions for a man at the height of his development or just past adolescence, starting with the smallest unit, the thickness of a finger. In his system the size of the head was one-sixth of the total height of the body, and this could only be shown when no extreme movement distorted its lines. The *Doryphorus* or *Spear Bearer* (pp. 21, 148), the *Diadoumenus*, his forehead bound with a fillet of victory, as the Greek name indicates, and the barely adult *Kyniskos* are therefore all shown in the same position—upright, one foot on tiptoe, the other flat on the ground—as if they had just stopped walking. The legs are slightly bent, the body pivots almost imperceptibly at the waist, the chest is exposed by the movement of the arms, the shoulders are tilted—one higher than the other—and the head is modestly lowered. This was how the harmony of the machine that is the human body could be seen most clearly—without a trace of movement. Although Polyclitus' figures are the product of theory, they are alive. In their reserve and detachment they become abstract symbols of human beings, exactly the effect he wanted.

One of Polyclitus' most admired works was of a woman: the *Wounded Amazon*, dedicated at Ephesus. It was generally supposed to be because of this statue, although it is arguable, that Polyclitus beat Phidias and the sculptor Kresilas in a competition. The Amazon does not differ from the other figures we have been describing as much as we might expect. Her stance is almost the same and her martial character enabled Polyclitus to provide the young woman with an almost virile strength.

Although Polyclitus always worked from the same principle, there is a noticeable line of development in his sculpture: for instance, the *Diadoumenus* is more supple than the *Doryphorus*. This was the result of Polyclitus' more direct observation of nature, but it may also have been partly inspired by the sculptor's stay in Athens shortly before 430 B.C.

Polyclitus must have met Phidias there. An Athenian by birth, Phidias had a lot of experience behind him and was at the height of his career. As a young man, in about 470 B.C., he had produced an enormous gilt wood and marble statue of Athena for the small city of Plataea. Its size and his use of contrasting colours anticipated the chryselephantine statue he was later to make for the Parthenon (p. 57). He also worked in Delphi (the thirteen statues of a monument in honour of Miltiades were said to be his). Then came the *Albani Kore*, the *Cassel Apollo*, and the *Cherchel Demeter*, although it has not been possible to work out in what order they were produced. We have only copies of these works, and they are not all equally good. In 454 B.C. Phidias finished a huge bronze Athena: the martial *Promachus* that stood on the Acropolis and could be seen from out at sea. A few years later he made another Athena (the *Athena Lemnia*) for the Acropolis, unwarlike this time, which was commissioned by the Athenian settlers of Lemnos. At about the same time he cooperated in decorating the Eleusis Telesterion where the Eleusinian Mysteries were celebrated; and, although it may not be his, the famous relief known as *Triptolemus between Demeter and Kore* (p. 131) undoubtedly reflects his influence. In 448 B.C., on the initiative of his friend Pericles, Phidias took control of the

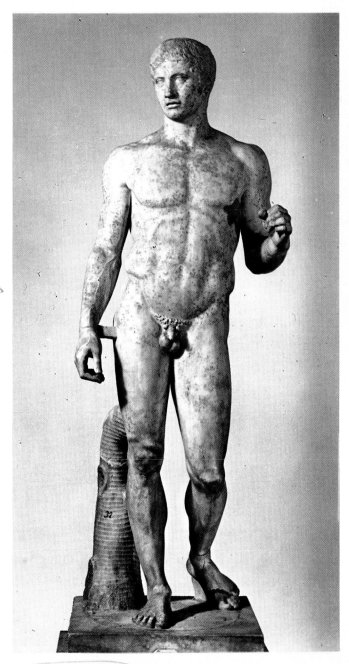

*Polyclitus,* Doryphorus, *c. 450–440* B.C. *(Roman copy). Naples, National Archeological Museum (p. 148).*

enormous undertaking to restore the Acropolis. Working with artists drawn from every corner of Greece by his fame, he launched a program of work that continued under his directorship for about fifteen years. It was not completed until after his death, but it was to make Athens the artistic capital of Greece. When proceedings instituted against him by Pericles' enemies forced him to go into exile, the crowning glory of his career came: the huge gold and ivory *Zeus of Olympia*, which his contemporaries regarded as his masterpiece. This was the extraordinary career of a man who, on top of all the administrative and organizational work he did for Pericles, left no artistic technique untried.

Phidias also painted, though admittedly in a very desultory manner. He was not an architect in the true sense of the word, but it is almost certain that Ictinus and Callicrates took his advice when they were building the Parthenon. It was possibly Phidias who decided on the position and appearance of the other buildings that continued to be erected on the Acropolis until the end of the fifth century. He solved the problems presented by the casting of the enormous *Athena Promachus*, carved the gold and ivory of the huge Zeus and Athena chryselephantines, and although he obviously did not personally carve all the marble friezes and pediments on the Parthenon, the credit for making the most important pieces as well as conceiving the whole brilliant design must undoubtedly go to him.

The decoration on the Parthenon is our only surviving example of his work, since everything else disappeared before the end of Antiquity, in particular the colossal statues of *Zeus* and the *Athena Parthenos*, which would have been marvellous to see in the original. No good copy of either of these works has survived and we only have a gem, a gold medallion, and some coins to give us some idea of the expression of tranquil nobility on the faces of these statues. Although the two statues broke with

tradition, we know they were regarded as cult images and that, because of their enormity (which made them clearly visible through the wide-open temple doors), they took up the whole end of the naos. Zeus was seated, but he was so huge that, had he been standing, his head would have gone through the ceiling of the building. Athena was standing, holding out to her people a life-size statue of Victory on her outstretched right hand. The god's throne and the goddess's helmet and sandals were decorated with figures that commemorated the glory of the immortals and the Greeks who served them and that symbolized the mysterious forces that warded off evil. The dramatic contrast between the brilliant gold of the clothes and the white ivory used for the uncovered parts of the body, as well as the statues' enormous size, must have given the group a somewhat barbaric appearance. The Greeks' growing contact with the East had given them this taste for the luxurious and the colossal, which had been neglected since the beginning of the Archaic period. But, according to all reports, the main impression the two statues gave was one of true divine majesty.

In spite of the extent of the damage they have suffered, the reliefs that were carved on the tympana, on the entablature, and high along the walls of the Parthenon between about 448 and 435 B.C. give us an immediate idea of what the work of Phidias and his collaborators was like. The main pediment, at the east end, portrays Athena's miraculous birth, springing fully armed from Zeus' brain under Hephaestus' hammer. In the wings are members of the Olympian family, seated or lying down (pp. 134, 136, 138, 139). On the west side are Athena and Poseidon, surrounded by the legendary heroes of Attica. The goddess makes an olive tree burst from the ground, while the god retaliates by producing a salt spring. The heroes are there to decide, on the basis of the importance of their gifts,

22

to which of the two deities the country should belong and grant Athena the patronage of Attica. A Doric frieze runs around the temple above the colonnade. The east façade, which was the most visible, also portrays the immortals, and here they are shown fighting against the giants. But the three other sides took spectators into a less awe-inspiring world. We have the *Centauromachy* on the south (pp. 143–45), the *Amazonomachy* on the west, and on the north, by way of example—perhaps loaded with political allusion at a time when Pericles was trying to establish lasting peace—are the misfortunes that came in the wake of the Trojan war, affecting both victor and vanquished alike, immediately after the city was taken. Contrary to the rules of architecture, a second, Ionic, frieze runs high along the perimeter walls of the naos (the enclosed part of the building) under the roofed porticoes. This marble frieze records the progress of the procession that brought the Athenian people to the Acropolis every four years at the time of the Panathenaic festival to give the ancient statue of Athena the peplos that the noblest young girls of the city had embroidered for her (pp. 140–42).

As we can see, all these themes celebrated patriotism and piety, two ideas that were still inseparable at this time. The new element was the imaginary transposition that brought humans and immortals together. The people shown climbing the Acropolis with great ceremony do not, as they did in real life, come to the ancient temple where the effigy of their patroness was located: they are brought abruptly face to face with the assembled Olympians celebrating Athena's birth and are welcomed among them. And it is the heroes, in whose existence the Greeks firmly believed, who choose whether Athena or Poseidon is to be the patron of their state. Phidias did not forget the fact that there was a fundamental difference between the two races and that one had to worship and obey the other, but he believed that it was possible to establish a degree of familiarity between creatures possessing the gift of reason, if everyone stayed in his prescribed place. Undoubtedly inspired by Eleusinian doctrine, he therefore gave deserving members of the human race a glimmer of hope, a glimpse of the possibility of entering the world of the gods. Inspiration of this order was backed by an art whose creative power is comparable to that of a Michelangelo. The whole composition, as well as each individual figure, is alive, and there is no perceptible effort in any of his work. Phidias disregarded everything that stood in the way of his genius with the serene confidence of the gods he portrayed: blind regard for tradition, technical virtuosity, and preoccupation with unnecessary detail. The strong blast of innovation swept all convention aside.

The sculptors we have just discussed were not the only ones at this period who deserve recognition, although they were the most important. The second half of the fifth century saw the rise of a whole galaxy of artists, but at this point we can do no more than run through their names. Kresilas (a native of Crete) was the sculptor of an idealized portrait of Pericles, of which there are several copies; Agoracritus produced a statue of Nemesis for the sanctuary of Rhamnus on the outskirts of Athens; Callimachus, who excelled in carving, was called "precious" because of the overrefinement of his work; and finally Alcamenes, possibly the most original, who kept close to Phidias' precepts but whose work contained a new sensitivity, as, for example, in the *Itys and Procne* group (the original of the *Borghese Ares* is attributed to him as well).

If Myron does not appear to have had followers, perhaps because of his attachment to the past, Polyclitus' influence, which was to make such a deep impression on the following centuries, did not have an immediate impact, at least not in sculpture.

Phidias' influence, on the other hand, was felt immediately in the almost mass-produced works that flooded Attica from about 430 B.C. onwards. Becoming redundant when the decoration of the Parthenon was finished, the craftsmen Phidias had worked with were employed by private individuals to carve reliefs on gravestones (the practice of erecting votive pillars to mark the spot where people were buried had been resumed after a long lapse). Often technically excellent, these steles were made during more than three-quarters of the fourth century and depicted the person who had died, sometimes alone but more often surrounded by his close friends, saying goodbye before the great journey. The most famous is the one commemorating the young Hegeso (c. 410 B.C.), showing a maid handing her a casket of jewels for the last time. Another portrays a mother with her newborn baby. Gradually, under the influence of changing ideas about the next world, the design became more elaborate, and often a whole family would be gathered around the deceased inside an architectural framework resembling a temple façade. At the same time the serenity that had characterized the earliest works was replaced by an increasingly uncontrolled and anguished expression of suffering on the faces of those who were about to depart this world.

After Phidias' death, and in particular after the long and gruelling war that had come to an end in 404 B.C. with the defeat of Athens, the mood changed drastically, not only in the city but in the entire Greek world. Patriotism lost much of its strength; people's faith in the gods was shattered by questioning philosophers and poets like Euripides; the economic situation worsened everywhere, and neither political nor religious communities could any longer afford to give artists the huge commissions of the past. Official optimism was expressed in Attic art for the last time in about 410, in the graceful figures of winged Victories that were carved on the balustrade running around the Temple of Athena Nike at the extreme west of the Acropolis. The figures are young, vibrant, totally charming and full of fun, such as the extremely famous one shown unlacing her sandals. Their transparent tunics do not quite conceal the beautiful naked bodies beneath, and this was a considerable innovation.

When the Athenian state commissioned Cephisodotus in 374 B.C. to produce a statue to mark the end of the war between Athens and other Greek cities, the sculptor did not create a commemorative work but an allegorical image representing Peace, a woman lost in thought, tenderly holding the child Plutus (the personification of plenty) in her arms. It is an important work in many respects, not only because it expresses the Greeks' weariness after so many exhausting wars, but because it also demonstrates a new interest in weaker creatures and a new trend towards the sentimental in official art. Until then, it had been apparent only in minor works intended for private individuals, such as the funerary lecythi decorated by the "Reed Painter" at the end of the fifth century.

## The Fourth Century and the Hellenistic Period

The period that came immediately after the Peloponnesian War is often regarded as no more than a transition between two different aspects of Classicism. However, we see it as more a very distinct break between two very different moods. As far as sculpture is concerned, the past had certainly not been forgotten, as is clear from the monuments that were built in several parts of the Peloponnesus during the first half of the fourth century. The subjects illustrated in the Bassae temple friezes are hackneyed and, in their somewhat provincial coarseness, still close to the Parthenon tradition. Their clothes billowing in the wind, the mounted Amazon and Nereid acroteria made by Timotheus for the Temple of Asclepius at Epidaurus (p. 160) are more original and freer in style. But the ones that are undeniably original are the figures on the pediments of the Tegea temple (*c.* 370 B.C.). These are the work of Scopas, a sculptor of exceptional talent and of great importance to the art of the fourth century.

Scopas came from Paros, and, although he started his career in the Peloponnesus, like Timotheus and so many others he undoubtedly had to look for work elsewhere, mainly in Asia Minor, since an impoverished Greece could not continue to guarantee her artists a living. Upon leaving, he could no longer command complete control of his projects, as he had at Tegea, where he both designed and decorated the temple. However, he cooperated in producing the large frieze running around the monumental sepulcher that was built at Halicarnassus for Mausolus, the prince of Caria (pp. 146–47), in about 350 B.C. A few years later at Ephesus, where a new temple in honour of Artemis was being built, Scopas carved a scene on the bottom drum of one of its columns; it undoubtedly portrays a burial rite, since the figures include Hermes, the deity who escorted souls to the underworld.

Scopas' reputation resulted in a commission to make an allegorical statue of Desire (the *Pothos*) for Samothrace. He also worked in other places, but we have very little detailed knowledge about this work. Nevertheless, we must mention his figure of a maenad dancing in wild Dionysiac ecstasy. A small copy of it in the museum of Dresden shows he had no qualms about portraying powerful emotion. This was a feature of his character, undoubtedly emphasized by his contact with the East, but it was already evident at the beginning of his career when he produced the east pediment of the Tegea temple (the only one that has partially survived). The subject, inspired by local legend, is dramatic, showing Heracles and Meleager (the archetypal heroes pursued by fate) taking part in hunting the Calydonian boar. The heads of the two figures have survived. Each is strong and powerful, with determined chin, marked bone structure, low forehead, tortured expression, and eyes deep set beneath arched brows. All trace of Classical serenity has disappeared, and the figures submit to a will beyond their control. The Mausoleum relief figures that are attributed to Scopas, too, are all gripped by powerful emotion.

The Mausoleum is a strange monument and shows how its Greek creators brought a foreign element into their work, although they had to follow a prearranged design and please the customer. We can see this clearly when we look at the statues of Mausolus and his wife. They are genuine portraits, clearly individual, with none of the idealization that sublimates the face of Kresilas' portrait of Pericles. The "barbarian" influence is also apparent in the friezes, though not quite so obviously, and, since Mausolus admired Hellenism, the subjects are taken from the most traditional Greek legends, for example, the Amazonomachy. But in order to satisfy the Oriental taste for historical anecdote, and at the same time because they had to fill the enormous area at their disposal, the sculptors engaged to decorate the monument (besides Scopas, they included Bryaxis, Timotheus, and Leochares, the presumed sculptor of the *Apollo Belvedere*) had weakened their work and had not always managed to avoid repetitive motifs. Although the work shows that the artists were technically very skilled, the composition lacks some discipline and is to a certain extent monotonous.

During the second third of the fourth century the reputation of the Athenian sculptor Praxiteles outstripped that of all other sculptors, including Scopas. He did not collaborate in decorating any monuments in Asia Minor (there were many others besides the Mausoleum, which was the most famous), but his customers came from all over the Greek world. He did not have an epic mind and confined himself to producing statues, showing no interest in either war or athletics. His objectives coincided with the urbane tastes of the upper classes to which he belonged. The gods he portrayed on a great many occasions were not the strongest or the wisest. He chose the youngest, the most attractive, and the most strikingly beautiful models that he could, and he gave them such names as Artemis, Apollo (who had very little in common with Homer's robust character), Eros, and, even more often, Aphrodite. There is no sense of the divine in his work, no claim that he is trying to portray the perfect human being. He carved his somewhat effeminate young men (he also produced a *Hermaphrodite*) and beautiful women to give visual and sensual pleasure. More often than not his subjects are portrayed completely naked, as is the *Cnidian Aphrodite*. Except for his statues of adolescents, Praxiteles' figures are physically well developed. The head, perched on an elongated neck, is generally small. His female figures have luxuriant, elaborate hairstyles, contrasting with and underlining the slenderness and delicacy of their remote, impassive faces.

But these great names and monumental works should not make us overlook how busy small workshops and independent artists were throughout the fourth century, working for private customers who were apparently less affected than public bodies by the economic malaise of the time.

During this period a great many Greeks, Athenians in particular, showed their gratitude to a deity for some favour they had received by dedicating reliefs or putting up votive pillars on their graves. The craftsmen who specialized in this genre did not reject new trends, which we see gradually creeping into their work, but they generally stayed close to the spirit of the fifth century, almost all of them excelling in a technique that was a direct derivative of the Parthenon tradition. It was also thanks to these commissions from private individuals or groups that portraiture developed during this period and went on to become increasingly popular. The portraits were at first those of famous men, commemorated by their admirers (Silanion's portrait of Plato should be mentioned in particular). Then came imaginary portraits of historical figures who had been dead for a long time, for example Homer, but whose appearance artists tried to reconstruct on the basis of their work. Finally ordinary family portraits appeared. The popularity of portraiture can be explained partly by the decline of the polis and the consequent more important role of the individual, but also partly by influence from Asia where, as is clear in the case of the Mausoleum, there was a cult of personality. Nevertheless, while they did their best to achieve a good likeness, Greek artists tried at the same time to link their portrait to a more general type (as Cresilas had done), unlike the Romans, who were to concentrate on minute detail.

One of the most famous of these portraits was Lysippus' depiction of Alexander the Great, and this was due as much to the fame of its subject as to the talent of its artist. There are so many copies of this work that it is not easy to tell what the original Alexander was like: the copies were made at different times and they vary accordingly (the most recent were probably made a long time after Alexander's death). The romantic portraits that were inspired by the legend that quickly sprang up around the hero are all hopelessly inaccurate. He must, however, have looked rather like the bust known as *Alexander Azara*. Its somewhat arid precision and determined expression appear to have been inspired by firsthand observation.

This precision, which was characteristic of bronze casting, was one of Lysippus' qualities. He came from the Peloponnesus, and, although he was self-taught, his work followed in the tradition of his predecessor Polyclitus. Like him he had a taste for athletics, and his most famous statue portrayed a standing young man using his right arm to rub himself with a strigil (a metal instrument for scraping off dust and sweat after violent physical exercise). It is called the *Apoxyomenus*, from the Greek word describing this particular action. The figure is sturdy but supple, and the elongation of the legs and the reduction of the head to one-seventh of the total height mark the beginning of a new system of proportions that is more willowy than the one used by Polyclitus. The torso pivots markedly on the hips, the movement of the arm lifts and brings the shoulders forward, the head is turned to the right. Lysippus' great contribution lay in realizing how arbitrary was the customary division of the body into front, side, and back. There is normally never such a marked jump between different planes, and the eye follows the curve of the flank towards the chest, or the transition from nape to neck, in one continuous movement. A statue by Lysippus can be looked at from all sides: the play of light, the effects of the contrast between shadow and gleaming bronze, the accuracy of the contours, all give an illusion of reality from whatever angle we look at it. One of the most successful works in this respect is *Hermes Tying His Sandal* (sometimes known as *Jason*).

Lysippus was very prolific, and his impact was almost immediate. Some of his work was on a large scale, as for example the monument known as *Alexander's Hunt*. This sarcophagus has incorrectly been called the *Alexander Sarcophagus* although it actually belonged to a Sydonian prince (as a matter of fact, the great conqueror is also taking part in the fighting). The dramatic battle scene depicted on the walls is clearly the work of Lysippus.

Archeologists usually put the beginning of the Hellenistic period at about this time—the last quarter of the fourth century. As mentioned earlier, this period was hardly different from the one that had just ended or from the one that followed, when the Roman empire spread throughout the whole Mediterranean basin. The polis had been an empty shell for years and no longer gave artists commissions of any importance, so they had to rely on the generosity of private individuals and even more on that of Asiatic princes. Religion had long before ceased to be the main, if not the only, source of inspiration, and sculptors had for years been going abroad to work in Asia. When Alexander died, the rulers of the large kingdoms that were subsequently set up became keen on collecting beautiful works of art, but this did not lead to any new artistic development. The wealth of these kings and their retinues ensured commissions, but for a long time there was no significant spiritual change. It was clearly apparent that Greece was no longer the focal point that it had been for so long. Even Athens was no more than a museum-city; its reputation was still very great but it was living on its past.

The torch was taken up by new cities, the capitals of the kingdoms that Alexander's successors had divided among themselves. The fact nevertheless remains that the predominant taste throughout the huge territories that Alexander had annexed to Greece stayed academic, closely tied to traditional subject matter and technique. Later we shall discuss works that should be regarded as revolutionary,

27

although when they appeared they were probably less popular than the countless copies of works by Polyclitus and Praxiteles. Not that these copies were all worthless—and our admiration of the *Venus de Milo* is indicative of this—but more often than not they lacked originality and their technique was no more than a virtuoso exercise.

The enormous numbers of terra cottas that were produced in various manufacturing centers scattered throughout the Greek world (the one at Mirina was far from the only one) confirm the public's taste for eroticism, elegance, and a slightly affected and childish sentiment, and this was also evident in works in marble. Most of the customers were in fact middle class and did not greatly appreciate originality. A further point to remember is that the buyers were all Greek emigrés (particularly at the beginning) who lived cut off from the local people, establishing no cultural contact with them for a long time. The two women Theocritus describes walking through festive Alexandria (in an Idyll written at the end of the fourth century) are not Egyptian but Greek. It was only gradually that the conquerors' descendants let themselves be influenced by the customs and feelings of the countries in which they had settled.

There was a great deal of difference among these various countries. In the Egypt of the Ptolemies, Alexandria rapidly became the economic and cultural center of the Mediterranean world. Monuments, undoubtedly decorated with many sculptures, sprang up everywhere, but they were subsequently destroyed or disappeared under buildings that were constantly being erected on the same sites. So all we can do is guess what their art (known as Alexandrian) was like, without really being able to describe it. Bas-reliefs illustrating typical landscapes with palm trees and crocodiles, the famous statue symbolizing the Nile, all these leave us in no doubt as to where they come from.

Nevertheless, was it here that "landscape relief" developed? The genre was very popular during the whole Hellenistic period. In it nature was shown independent of man, possessing an importance it had never been accorded by Greek art. The Egyptians' well-known love of caricature leads us to identify as Alexandrian some extremely realistic figures of wrinkled old women (sometimes still holding a bottle they have just emptied), grotesque female dancers, wretched creatures with tiredness written all over their faces and bodies—these were the types that figurine makers liked, although they were also portrayed in large-scale sculpture.

We are on surer ground when we turn our attention to Pergamum, the capital built in the middle of Asia Minor shortly after Alexander's death, by Attalus, the founder of an energetic dynasty who used artists to commemorate his achievements. In about 228 B.C. the king dedicated a monument here, which depicted figures with the typical appearance and pronounced ethnic features of the tribes he had just conquered—Persians and Gauls, as well as Amazons and giants—so as to connect his victory with deeds from mythology. The figures lie dead on the ground, portrayed with maximum realism: mouths open, eyes blank, faces contorted in suffering, hair dishevelled. But the most important monument (and fortunately we have numerous figures from it) was the frieze carved on the Pergamene altar base (*c.* 180 B.C.). It was 120 meters (390 feet) long and had been dedicated to Athena and Zeus by Eumenes to commemorate his father's victory (pp. 166–67). The colossal work is enormously high and portrays the war between the gods and giants. The fighting is fierce and the figures are furiously entangled in the hubbub of battle. The violence is evident not only in the movement but in the contorted facial expressions as well; some of the figures are shown screaming, mouths wide open. The human figures are joined by monsters (snake-like from the waist down) and there are also wild animals taking part in the battle. It is an undoubtedly romantic composition, impressive for all its atrocities—the undisputed peak of Hellenistic art. However the Pergamum school also went in for smaller and quieter works, and it was this school rather than its rival at Alexandria that produced the charming and poetical landscape reliefs we have mentioned earlier.

Lesser Hellenistic schools flourished in several parts of the ancient world, each with its own distinct character. The Rhodes school, whose artists had in fact collaborated in the Pergamene altar frieze, is known to us mainly through one masterpiece: the *Nike of Samothrace*, dating from the beginning of the second century (p. 172). The winged figure brings storm-tossed seas to mind, but the excitement is more controlled than at Pergamum.

It is very difficult to say exactly when the history of Greek sculpture ends. The Greek spirit, which was very different from the spirit behind Roman art, survived long after the formerly Hellenic territories had fallen under Roman rule. At the time of the Emperor Hadrian there was in fact an important Classical renaissance, when sculptors enthusiastically returned to purer models, to a certain extent disregarding the innovations of the Hellenistic period. Drawing inspiration from these models, they produced works that may not be very original but are among the most beautiful items that have survived, such as, for example, the statue of Antoninus. But the inspiration dried up, and even though Greek art was later to experience another period of greatness in the Byzantine age, sculpture was not involved in this second renaissance.

*Dying Gaul (detail), Hellenistic art,*
c. *228* B.C. *(Roman copy).*
*Rome, Capitoline Museum.*
*The bronze original, together with other statues of Gauls and Persians, decorated the top of Attalus I's monument on the Pergamum acropolis, commemorating the king's victory over the Galatians of Moesia and the peoples of Persia.*

# MATERIAL
# AND COLOUR

Then first he form'd the immense and solid
shield;
Rich various artifice emblazed the field;
Its utmost verge a threefold circle bound;
A silver chain suspends the massy round;
Five ample plates the broad expanse
compose,
And godlike labours on the surface rose.
This done, what e'er a warrior's use required
He forg'd; the cuirass that outshone the fires,
The greaves of ductile tin, the helm impress'd
With various sculpture, and the golden crest.

(Homer, *Iliad*, Book XVIII: "Vulcan Forges
Achilles' Shield." Translation by Alexander
Pope.)

The colour illustrations on pages 33 through 64, which are listed below together with page references to explanatory captions, serve basically as an introduction to the living world of sculpture. It is not simply a world of three dimensions, it is one of colour as well, since a three-dimensional object is made of materials that have various chromatic qualities and stands in a natural or artificial environment that lends it further colour. The purpose of the illustrations and captions on pages 80 through 174, however, is to instruct, and we have there the essential ideas, arranged in chronological order, for a thorough understanding of the colour and black-and-white works illustrated in the two sections.

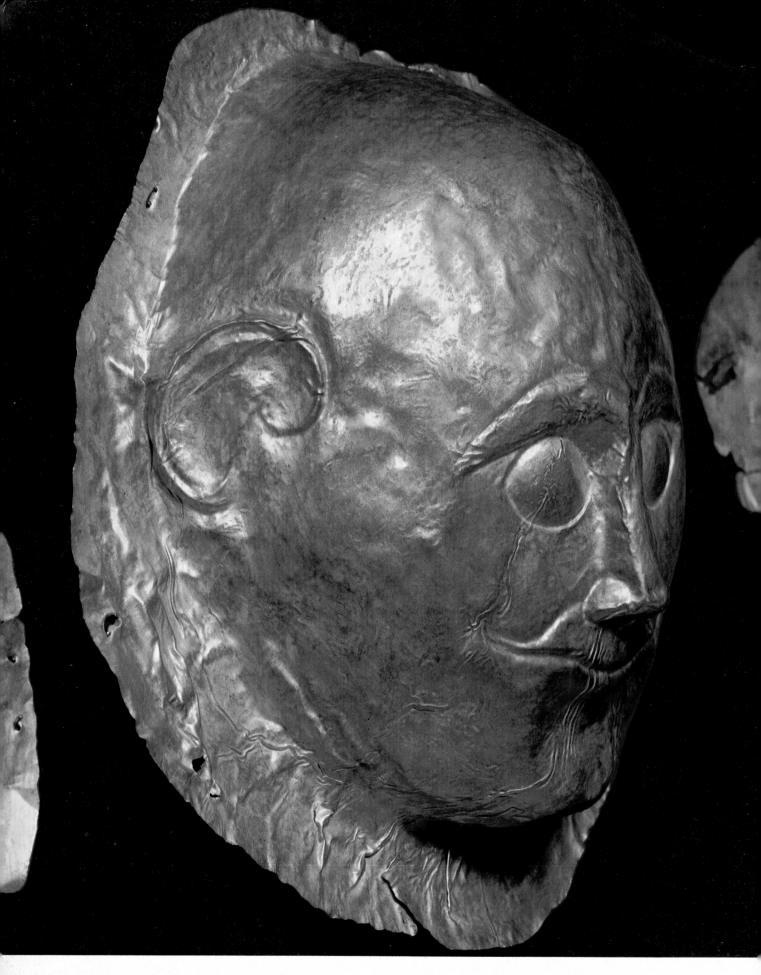

51

In any society works of art are produced according to theoretical principles and practical rules that form the sum of the intuition and experience an artist has acquired through his own imagination and the requirements of the people he works for. The sculptor at work is the private, determining occasion of a public act, his personal contribution to the cultural and historical heritage.

Page 65: *Sculptor Carving a Herma*, base of "red-figure" vase attributed to Epithetus, *c.* 510 B.C. Copenhagen, Nationalmuseet.

# THE ARTIST-CRAFTSMAN

Phidias was a craftsman, the best public worker in his art. Do you imagine that he did not know this beautiful that you speak of? Because he did not make the eyes of his Athena of gold, nor the rest of her face, nor her hands and feet. But he made them of ivory; ivory is also beautiful.

(Plato, *Dialogues*, "Great Hippias," 4th century B.C.)

What did sculpture mean to those who saw it living and changing and to those who created it? And after all this time are our reasons for admiring it the same as those of the Ancient Greeks?

The importance of sculpture to Greek civilization was not determined simply by the presence or absence of abundant deposits of high-quality marble; in some places where there were marble deposits, other materials were initially sculpted. The Pentelic quarries near Athens, those of Paros and Naxos in the Cyclades, and others on Thasos and in Asia Minor undoubtedly supplied sculptors with large quantities of the stone they needed, but many of the earliest works come from Crete and the Peloponnesus where there was in fact no marble. If the mere presence of marble quarries must necessarily lead to sculpture, how do we explain the meagerness of sculptural output in Cretan and Mycenaean civilizations, at least after the glittering period of greatness in the third millennium when the Cycladic idols were produced?

In any case, we should not be taken in by the fact that most of the works that have survived—both free-standing and relief—are made either of marble or of a variety of soft limestone known as poros. Statues were very often made of bronze, and the greatest artists, such as Polyclitus, Lysippus, and many others, were primarily, if not exclusively, bronze casters. But, as mentioned earlier, in periods of scarcity their work was melted down so that the metal could be used again. Greek sculptors also employed other valuable or fragile materials, and these inevitably had a short lifespan.

Terra cotta was used to make other things besides small figurines, and the Olympian group portraying Ganymede being carried off by Zeus (p. 51) is only one of many other large works (now lost) that were made of clay. Many monumental friezes were also made of clay, as for example the sixth-century friezes of Larissa in Asia Minor. We know that wood was used a great deal in the Archaic period, although sometimes the carved image would be covered in bronze sheet metal, as in the three statuettes that were found a few years ago at Dreros on the island of Crete. The enormous statue of Athena made by the young Phidias for the city of Plataea had a gilt wood body and a plaster head. Gold and ivory, both imported, were enormously popular at the end of the seventh century and the beginning of the sixth, long before Phidias had combined them in his Parthenon and Olympia statues.

If it is obvious that no three-dimensional art can develop in a country without the necessary raw materials (at least this was not possible until the beginning of modern times), it is equally obvious that the nature of the soil alone cannot account for the astonishing flowering of Greek sculpture during the thousand years or so following the transition from the Bronze Age to the Iron Age. Nor can we believe the ill-considered opinion that sculptors were inspired by the brightness of the sky and the purity of a stark landscape.

To the extent that external circumstances (political, social, and so on) may play some part in the development of art, we have discussed the importance of magical and religious beliefs in the emergence and history of Greek sculpture. We shall see later on how much the city contributed to its success and what part the setting up of Hellenistic kingdoms played in its development. But the main point eludes analysis, and that is the character and temperament of the peoples who settled in the Balkan peninsula and its surrounding islands at about the beginning of the first millennium. For some of the features that make up the specific character of sculpture can also be found in other expressions of the Hellenic genius.

The most striking is the fact that the Greeks were interested primarily in the human being. Perhaps this is where we might find some reflection of the natural environment in which the Greeks lived. They had a temperate climate, a poor soil, but one that could be made productive by hard work; sweeping views over seas that were often stormy, but there were islands dotted all over and the winds were regular; the mountains closely bounding areas of land on the mainland itself did not form impassable barriers. It was nothing like Egypt, with its vast stretches of desert scorched by a merciless sun. The Greeks felt at home everywhere, in a world that seemed to have been made on their scale, a world that could be ruled only by gods who resembled and understood them.

The environment was so amenable and so suited to man's needs that he hardly gave it a thought. There was no need to fight it or try to control it. It was undoubtedly very pleasant to lie in the shade of a plane tree, as Socrates did to talk to Phaedrus; the olive grove praised by the chorus of *Oedipus at Colonus* was also very pleasant. But these were such ordinary things that they hardly deserved a show of surprise, much less a closer look. However, the barbarians, whose lands had been annexed to Greece by Alexander's colonial expansion, lived in an environment that dwarfed them. They were therefore the first to give man his proper unassuming position in the world and to use landscapes as a context for their works of art. Until then, Greek art had deliberately ignored nature. Though a landscape could not really be constructed around a statue, it could have been done in relief sculpture, but the Greeks did not even try.

The battles illustrated in Greek friezes take place outside a living context, against a neutral background in which the withered trees and strangely shaped rocks we sometimes come across are not shown for their own sake. There is no attempt at likeness or realism, and the only importance of these objects is topographical, indicating that the episode is taking place outdoors. Indeed, when Phidias wanted to show that Athena and Poseidon had argued over possession of Attica on the actual spot on which the Parthenon had been built, he framed his portrayal of this episode on the west pediment between two neighbouring rivers, the Cephissus and the Illyssus. But the rivers he placed in the corners of the tympanum were no ordinary rivers flowing between banks, although undoubtedly he would have been technically capable of showing this; they were human personifications. The same thing was done when the east pediment of the temple at Olympia was being decorated. Clearly no attempt was made to create by means of a background what we today would call atmosphere. The only thing that counted was the human being.

Greek artists showed equally little interest in the animal world, and they brought it into their art only when it had something to do with man and his interests. It had undoubtedly occupied an important place in the early development of three-dimensional art, and we have already mentioned the bronze of terra-cotta horses and oxen that were found buried beneath the oldest sanctuaries, but, as belief in the magical value of such substitutes grew weaker and when centers of art moved to the cities (where animal rearing certainly had no place), these figurines gradually decreased in number. Later on, genuine statues of cattle may have been dedicated as votive offerings—this was undoubtedly the case of Myron's *Cow* for the Athens Acropolis—although more often than not we know nothing about the circumstances in which these offerings took place.

Generally speaking, sculptors portrayed animals for two reasons. They were either wild animals and animallike monsters from the East—lions, panthers, griffons, chimeras, sphinxes, and so on—which were shown either in their mythological role as victims of legendary heroes (admittedly much

Horseman's Grave Monument,
*Attic art, beginning of the 4th century* B.C.
*Athens, National Museum.*

less often in relief than in painting) or possessing a symbolic or protective importance, as in the case of the lions standing on the battlefields of Anpholus and Chaeronea. Or they were domestic animals, closely linked to the character of the human being with whom they were portrayed. The winner of a race could not be shown without the horse that had actually won it for him; while on gravestones a dog was always portrayed with its master, as was the little slave who was so often shown huddled in a corner. As for the figurines of hares, cockerels, and small birds that lovers gave one another as presents, these were mere objects with no life of their own. This is not to say that artists produced animal figures without care or skill. Their horses in particular are sometimes magnificent pieces of sculpture, the embodiments of nobility and passion.

Human form was the only one the Greek deities had assumed, and they were thus portrayed in Greek art. The forces ruling the world were never given the monstrous appearance that some of them had in Egypt or in the East. Unlike Horus, Apollo did not have the head of a hawk, nor Hera the head of a cow. Dionysius may indeed have been called the Bull, but he was always portrayed as a human, and the power Artemis had over wild animals was indicated solely by the presence of the tamed beasts standing by her side. The only creatures that were shown as a combination of various different species were the unimportant ones there was never any question of worshiping (such as the centaurs or the Minotaur), or ones that were traditionally portrayed in this way or had been imported from abroad. And the only reason these were portrayed at all was so that they could be shown being destroyed by members of a civilization protected by the immortals.

Because man's skilled hands were capable of carrying out the most difficult of tasks, because he was the only creature in the whole of creation who knew how to develop the qualities of his mind and body, and even more because he was the only one who had the gift of reason, the human being was the only creature that genuinely mattered as far as the Greeks were concerned. And if the gods possessed a fraction of the power they jealously refused to grant the human race, they had to be portrayed in the form of creatures like ourselves, but freed if not from feelings at least from the physical ills afflicting human beings—disease, old age, and death. Sophocles may have been the first to formulate it, but the idea that man is one of the most marvellous wonders of the world was as old as the Greek people itself. It was implicit in Homer's poems, and right from the start it was also the inspiration behind sculpture.

Homeric heroes were often said to be "like gods," and the Greeks' ambition was in fact to come as close as possible to the perfection the gods embodied without in any way arousing their jealousy. This would explain the impersonal nature of so many figures and why it is so difficult for us to distinguish between representations of humans and gods, particularly in the long line of *korai* and *kouroi*.

The religious beliefs current in Egypt dictated that when an artist made a funerary statue he would try to obtain the best possible likeness (as, for example, in the *Squatting Scribe*) so that the "double" of the person who had died would have no difficulty in recognizing the stone or wood substitute in which it had to live. But the approach of the Greek sculptor and his customers was totally different. The worshiper wanted to give to the god to whom he was dedicating his statue an ideal image of as perfect a being as possible. Is it likely that all the people commemorated by statues in cemeteries and sanctuaries would have been young, handsome, and strong? Their aim was to have themselves portrayed at their best, as they would have

liked to be in real life, in order to please the gods as well as the living who came to pay their respects at the graveside.

It is therefore not surprising that the facial expressions of works produced within individual workshops and schools had no distinguishing characteristics for such a long time. Even in the middle of the Classical period, when all the technical problems had been solved, a sculptor like Polyclitus gave his *Doryphorus* (p. 21), *Diadoumenus*, and even the much younger *Kyniskos* not only identical expressions of religious seriousness, but more or less the same facial features and the same size and build.

This was one of the reasons why portraiture appeared so late in Greek art—not until the fifth century, in fact. Yet, far from trying to get the strongest individual likeness as the Romans were to do, Greek artists only brought out those features that would make their figure the representative of the social and ethnic group to which he belonged. At the height of their development, as in the Archaic period, gravestones do not give us an individual likeness of the dead but a more general picture of, for example, a landowner playing with his dog, a young man (somewhat of an aesthete), smelling a flower, a hoplite, or a mother holding her child in her arms. The only thing that tells us who is buried in the grave is an inscription. The idealized character of Cresilas' Pericles portrait, which was produced when Pericles was still alive or shortly after his death, is quite evident. All trace of weariness and daily preoccupation lies completely hidden beneath the self-confident calmness befitting the head of a great state. And although when we look at the much later beautiful bronze head that was found on Delos (p. 174) we have the impression that the subject actually sat for the artist, it is the spirit of the merchant class ruling the sacred island at the beginning of the first century that emanates.

This notion is bound to surprise those who think of a portrait as a photographic reproduction, but it ties up with one of the basic principles of Hellenism. There is absolutely no doubt that nowhere else in the ancient world were human dignity and the individual more highly regarded than in Greece, but equally, nowhere else did the individual have such a deep awareness that he was nothing more than a component in a community—the polis—whose unity and cohesion he had to respect. A Greek was first and foremost a citizen. He knew that his liberty existed only to the extent that it did not infringe on the liberty of others and that he kept to his appointed place. The talents he had been given by the gods he proudly tried to exhibit to the best of his abilities (and nowhere else did contests of every kind stimulate the competitive spirit to the extent that they did in Greece), but they gave him a purely moral superiority over his countrymen and it would have shown inordinate sacrilege to use them to impose his authority over men who were his equals. There was genuine outrage among the citizenry when men like Alcibiades openly claimed that their extraordinary character placed them above the common law.

The painted or carved image was reserved for the gods, whether it portrayed the deities themselves or had been dedicated to them as an act of devotion. Until the fifth century, the Greeks believed that the more striking the likeness the greater the effectiveness of the image's magical value. Copying the features of a mere mortal therefore meant infringing on divine privilege. It was because they were regarded as true heroes (in the religious sense of the word) that statues of Harmodius and Aristogiton, who had tried to put the city on its feet again by reintroducing democracy, were erected within the sacred precincts of the Agora a few years after their deaths. And it was because Themistocles had saved his country that it was possible for his portrait (which has survived) to be carved. Though the primitive, magic idea that reproducing a person's image raised him to the ranks of those deserving worship disappeared within the course of two or three generations, enough of it was left to make sure that portraits never became too personal.

The body, which was much less individualized than the face, lent itself even more to the Greeks' concept of mankind. They believed that man had a right to be proud of his body since the gods had made it in their image. His duty was to develop and make it as perfect as possible for no other reason than to show his gratitude. Athletics was therefore more than a sport: it was a religious act, and its decline in the Hellenic world coincided with the decline of faith. It is therefore hardly surprising that the portrayal of the physically well-developed body had such a dominant place in the repertoire of free-standing sculpture. When statues were dedicated in a sanctuary or erected over a grave, the person commemorated would be shown as an athlete even if he had never distinguished himself by any athletic prowess. All the more reason why the victor of the games described in the last canto of the *Iliad*, which were held as much in honour of the immortals as in that of the important people who had recently died, should thank the gods who had ensured his success by dedicating a statue that showed him at the height of his strength and brilliance. More often than not such a statue would be commissioned and paid for not by the athlete but by his city, which shared in his glory. This then is the characteristically Greek idea that associated an individual's successes as well as his failures with the community of which he was a part (quite rightly in this particular case, since the community provided the champion's training). Sculptors therefore found these statues a source of practically guaranteed income, particularly since, thanks to the fame of some of these figures, their makers were even asked to go and work abroad.

Sculptors had other work besides commemorating famous athletes. They were commissioned to produce many different kinds of statues, since those in charge of the sanctuaries did not want to be accused of negligence any more than of an excessive adherence to the past. During the Classical period, many of the old statues the faithful still found perfectly acceptable no longer complied with current fashion and often had deteriorated in the course of time. These had to be restored, and during the fifth and fourth centuries artists were given a chance to show what they could do. When Greece became poor the market widened considerably, and sculptors who could no longer make a living in their own country turned their eyes to Asia Minor. Their new customers had different tastes; nevertheless, the human being continued to be portrayed. The athletically perfect body was now out of date and another type, introduced by Praxiteles and his successors, became fashionable, but the subject matter still revolved around man.

How did the Greeks see it? First of all, artists obviously attempted to produce works their public would find beautiful, but they always tried to understand how this beauty was formed and how the human body was made by taking its elements apart. With the sense of harmonious proportion that characterized Hellenism, artists tried right from the start to give the human body natural proportions, and they were soon able to position its various elements with accuracy. Although small-scale Egyptian sculpture set them on the right road, Greek sculptors must have analyzed the functioning of the muscles and different parts of the human body entirely on their own—since apparently no large statue from the Nile valley could have reached Greece at this period. Though they were unable to show this functioning very well at the beginning, they recognized its importance very early on, and the clumsy lines that score the back, stomach, and flanks of the marble Sunium *kouros* and other sculptures from the early Archaic period show how interested artists were in anatomy and the principles that make the human body work.

Greek sculpture had been inspired by a sense of order long before it culminated in Polyclitus' mathematical approach. One primary reason that sculptors concentrated on the human body for so long, to the almost total exclusion of everything else, was because the human body was better suited to analytical study, because its structure followed logical rules, and because each of its elements had a specific function. There was, however, no need for the body to be portrayed motionless, like the *kouroi* or the *Doryphorus*. Movement brought out the function and play of muscles to a much greater extent. The stance of the *Discobolus* may be physically impossible, but it does display the athlete's suppleness to perfection and with extraordinary realism. The mechanism of a body distorted by physical effort is completely revealed.

Although Greek sculptors always started from the same theoretical baseline, their main concern was always to produce lifelike works. The surprising thing is that they succeeded in this so well that the abstract nature of the underlying principle disappeared completely. Without being able to explain it, we might quite justifiably call this the Greek miracle.

The inspiration that brought these statues to life and ensured they did not remain abstract creations was also present in monumental sculptures. These could be either pedimental figures (at first in mid-relief, then, from the middle of the sixth century, always free-standing), or reliefs running above temple colonnades or along temple walls.

Apart from the often rather onerous constraints imposed by the architectural framework to which their composition had to adapt, artists had more freedom at their disposal when they chose subjects that did not force them to portray an act of religious piety with the accuracy demanded by a rite. However, this subject was not ignored in relief, and small slabs, sometimes 1 meter (3 feet) high, often portrayed a meeting between a god and a mortal (usually accompanied by his family), who is thanking the god for some favour. One of the earliest examples of this genre (found on the Acropolis) was made in honour of Athena (p. 48), and a great many of these slabs were dedicated by grateful patients to the physician Asclepius at his sanctuary in Epidaurus. A point to be remembered is that the same inspiration lies behind the scene in the Ionic frieze on the Parthenon, though it is on a much larger scale, in which the patroness of the city is being offered the veil woven for her by the daughters of the noblest Athenian families (p. 142). Though works of this kind are filled with piety because of the nature of the building they were intended for and though the ceremonies they portray had to be accurate from the point of view of ritual, they contain more supplementary characters and their realism is greater. The figures are not all identical, all frozen in the same stance in uncompromisingly straight lines, as they are in Oriental paintings and reliefs intended for the same purpose. Each figure has its own personality, which is brought out by different stances and movements. The difference between the Oriental and the Hellenistic styles had nothing to do with the requirements of religion, but was due to the distinct temperaments of the two civilizations.

Sculptors had even more freedom when the monumental relief did not portray a ceremony but narrative and action, and in practice this was almost always the case since the Panathenaic frieze was exceptional in all respects. When a building was to be decorated—and it was always a religious building like a temple or a tomb, such as the Lycian dynasty tomb at Xanthus or the Mausoleum at Halicarnassus—only subjects connected with the world of gods and heroes were chosen, the latter including those whose merit raised them above the rest of mankind, for example, the conquerors of Troy. More often than not the dead were raised to the rank of heroes.

Yet, even within this restricted sphere, not all mythological legends were equally important; some were completely ignored, even though vase paintings are indicative of their great popularity. It seems that, once the Archaic period was over, the legends that had been enjoyed before decreased in number. However, the success of the Gigantomachy, in which the whole Olympian family was triumphantly involved, never lessened. As early as the first third of the sixth century the Corfu pediment, for example, portrays Zeus striking one of his enemies with a thunderbolt; some fifty years later the Hekatompedon pediment shows Athena running Enceladus through with a spear; the metopes on the east side of the Parthenon portray the gods fighting with rebels; and one of the masterpieces of Hellenistic sculpture—the frieze running around the great Pergamum altar (c. 180 B.C.)—exuberantly tells the story of the decisive battle in which the Olympian gods were victorious (pp. 166–67). Heracles was one of the most important heroes and was famous throughout the Hellenic world, and it would be impossible to list the many representations of his exploits. Theseus came rather a long way behind him, and he was commemorated mainly in Attica (where he came from). Some local legends were illustrated only in their places of origin, and several of the legends carved on the metopes of the Silarus (modern Foce del Sele) temples, south of Paestum, are unknown. But the Trojan war and the Greeks' battles with the Amazons were illustrated countless times. These episodes had taken on a symbolic importance and represented real encounters with the invading barbarians of Asia. Although the Greeks had for a very long time played down the specifics of given facts by illustrating them in only a general way, the allusion was perfectly obvious. It was logical, too, in accordance with the Greek belief that art, like Aristotelian science, dealt only in the general.

This relative poverty in choice of subject matter is surprising when we think of the extraordinary richness of Greek mythology. For example, both Bellerophon and Perseus, who had been popular with a great many vase painters during the Archaic period, had an extraordinarily insignificant place in sculpture. However paradoxical this may seem, imagination was far from being the Greeks' predominant quality. Greek artists always boasted of following in the footsteps of their teachers, and they never seem to have regarded originality with anything but suspicion. To perfect what was already there; that was their aim. Reasons of ritual do not in themselves explain why some sculptural types were so rigid or why they lasted so long. Improving skills and methods only changed their outward appearance but did nothing to alter the underlying principles. Just as we find that the *kouroi* of the early Archaic period inspired Polyclitus' physically perfect statues and logically led to their development, so Phidias' gold-and-ivory Zeus was an embodiment of Homer's magnificent god, whose majesty early artists had tried to portray with their still very inadequate skills.

As for the battle scenes that formed the most common theme in monumental relief (regardless of who was involved), they were throughout antiquity always composed along the same lines: couples in hand-to-hand combat fighting over a dead or wounded figure. The movements were repeated. Though it was a long time before artists learned how to give an impression of depth by overlapping their figures—which was only a question of technique—there is as much impetuous excitement

*Apollonius and Tauriscus of Tralles,* Farnese Bull, *1st century* B.C. *(Roman copy). Naples, National Museum. The group portrays Antiope's sons torturing their persecutor Dirce. Found in Rome, in the Baths of Caracalla. From the Farnese Collection.*

in the Gigantomachy frieze on the Siphnian Treasury at Delphi (*c.* 525 B.C., pp. 44, 99, 101) as there is in the Bassae temple friezes produced 150 years later (if we accept the late date that has recently been put forward).

It is no exaggeration to say that Greek art would never have been what it was and would never have developed in the way it did without foreign influence. There can be no doubt about the important role the East played in the sudden flowering of Hellenic art just after the end of the seventh century. With the appearance of the *kouros* and *kore* types, statuary developed along Egyptian lines. And it is in eastern Greece, in Miletus and Samos, that we first see the heavy seated figures that were directly inspired by Asiatic art. However, it was not long before these imitations showed signs of a new, genuinely Hellenic character, and the assimilation was so total that originality developed at almost the same time. But the stimulus had come from outside.

It was again the East that, in the same way, introduced an almost radical change into Greek art towards the end of the fifth century. After Persia's defeat and the short period of Athenian supremacy, contacts between the two continents increased. The Greeks were dazzled by the luxury and wealth of the people they had conquered, and, for their part, the princes who ruled the small kingdoms of Asia Minor under the aegis of Alexander the Great were impressed by the Greeks' artistic achievements. (Classicism had not broken with the past. It was simply the mature and admittedly brilliant expression of ideas that had surfaced in previous periods. And if historical events had something to do with the development of Classicism, this was not the result of foreign influence but because at that time the whole of Greece suddenly became aware of its own strength after a succession of unexpected victories.)

Greek art reached its climax in the fifth century; the fourth century marked a break. The city structure disintegrated, people no longer believed in deities who had not been able to help their worshipers (as at the time of the Median wars, for example), and the Greeks' contact with the vast continent of Asia showed them how insignificant man was in comparison with nature and how mysterious were the forces ruling the world. An anxiety developed that Greece had never really known before. Deities that had until then been unknown—Adonis for example, who died and rose from the dead each year—replaced the self-confident gods who had for so long been regarded as the natural protectors of Greek civilization. Individuals who stood out from the crowd were regarded more highly, and it was at this point that the genre of portraiture began to develop. The very foundations of Greek thought crumbled, and naturally the same thing happened in art. We have already discussed how tormented Scopas' figures were, how far removed from the old conventions were the attractive young men and graceful young women carved by Praxiteles. The break with the past seemed even sharper than the one which occurred in the seventh century.

But the circumstances were completely different. In the seventh century Greek artists gave the impression of being novices. They did have something to say but they did not know how to set about expressing their aims, as had already been done in literature. So they had enthusiastically adopted new methods from Egyptian and Eastern civilizations, where they had discovered statuary and monumental relief, and learned how to be original themselves by copying work from abroad and using it as a starting point to develop in a direction that matched their character, their beliefs, and the social conditions in which they lived. In the fourth century the opposite happened. Greek sculptors had become so skilled that they were respected by the very nations from which their distant ancestors had tried to learn. They were invited to Asia to make items local artists were quite incapable of producing. They did not find new techniques there, since they were more accomplished than anyone else, but they did find an inspiration that was completely alien to the Greek spirit. They assimilated this inspiration and gave it Hellenic expression. "Let us form new thoughts with old verses," as an eighteenth-century poet put it, and Hellenistic sculpture showed that kind of transplantation. The techniques were traditional, but they revealed new tendencies that were Oriental rather than Hellenic.

We have seen that this kind of transplantation was not an absolute rule in the fourth century any more than it later was. It is apparent in such famous later works as the *Laocoön* group and the *Farnese Bull*, both of which display the bombastic yet touching overstatement that was so far removed from the moderation that had once been the norm. This transplantation is also apparent in the beautiful landscapes in which nature assumed an importance it had never known before. And if the study of anatomy stemmed directly from a long tradition, the inspiration behind the tempestuous Gigantomachy on the Pergamum altar frieze was the result of an absolutely original fusion of past and future trends. But there were countless statues that ignored these new developments and were based directly on masterpieces of the fifth century. Public taste had undeniably stayed the same for years, and it was during the second century that free copies of the greatest masterpieces began to be made. It was not until the end of the second century that the mechanical copying was introduced, using the painting process. The number of such copies was to increase during the Roman empire, and it is thanks to them that we are familiar with some of the works whose originals have disappeared.

Copies played an essential part in perpetuating the Greek ideal, and they were first discovered during the Renaissance. More came to light in the two centuries that followed. The coldness with which these copies had been infused by the skilled sculptors' assistants who had made them matched the somewhat academic taste of that period. The modern world was not to have any direct contact with antiquity until Archaic statues were excavated. The naïveté and garish colours of Archaic statuary would have shocked art lovers of the Renaissance. In fact, even when the marble was taken down from the Parthenon and sent to London by Lord Elgin, the contemporary public was rather surprised by its freshness and spontaneity, finding it insufficiently academic.

During the Hellenistic period, the two currents had therefore flowed side by side and in the same riverbed, if you will. This very coexistence was a mark of the unity of Greek art. However serious the break at the beginning of the fourth century may have been, however different the subsequent tendencies that crept in, they did not break with the aims of the great Archaic and Classical sculptors to the extent we might have expected. Even when it was forced to abandon its proud detachment from the world and to take account of nature, Greek art remained first and foremost a human art. And that is undoubtedly why more than twenty centuries later, in a world that is so completely different, it remains of fundamental importance to us.

# THE WORKS

Are you the Delian Apollo? Yes, I am.
Are you eighteen cubits high? Yes.
Made of gold? Yes, made of gold.
And unclad? Yes, only a belt goes around my
middle.
For what reason in your left hand do you
hold the bow
And in your right hand the Graces?
To hold back the stupid from being
insolent ...
And reward the good.

(Callimachus, fragment from the *Aetia*,
dialogue between the poet and the statue of
Apollo at Delos, 3rd century B.C.)

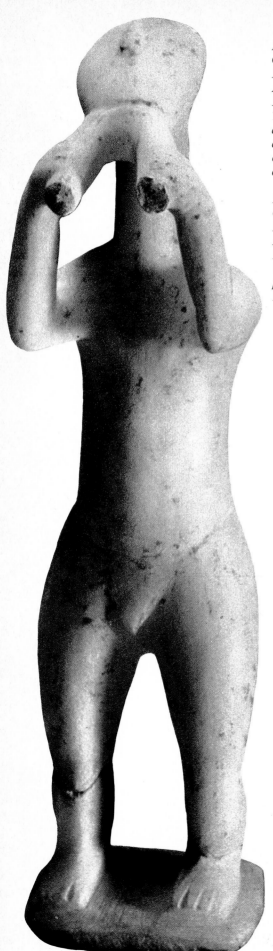

*Left:* Double-flute Player, *Cycladic art,* c. 2000 B.C. *Marble, height 3.2 in. Athens, National Archeological Museum. The function of this figure, which is almost certainly male, was to wake the dead in the next world. From the cemetery of the small Cycladic island of Keros.*

*Page 34:* Lyre Player, *Cycladic art,* c. 2000 B.C. *Marble, height 8.8 in. Athens, National Archeological Museum. The statuette was made for the same purpose as the one above. From Keros.*

*Below:* Idol, *Neolithic Cretan art,* c. 3000 B.C. *Terra cotta, height 3.6 in. Heraklion, Museum. Magical grave artifact portraying the stylized "violin-shaped" figure of the Mediterranean mother-goddess, whose enlarged hips were a symbol of fertility. The geometric zig-zag pattern carved on it is similar to decorative motifs on contemporary pottery. From Knossos.*

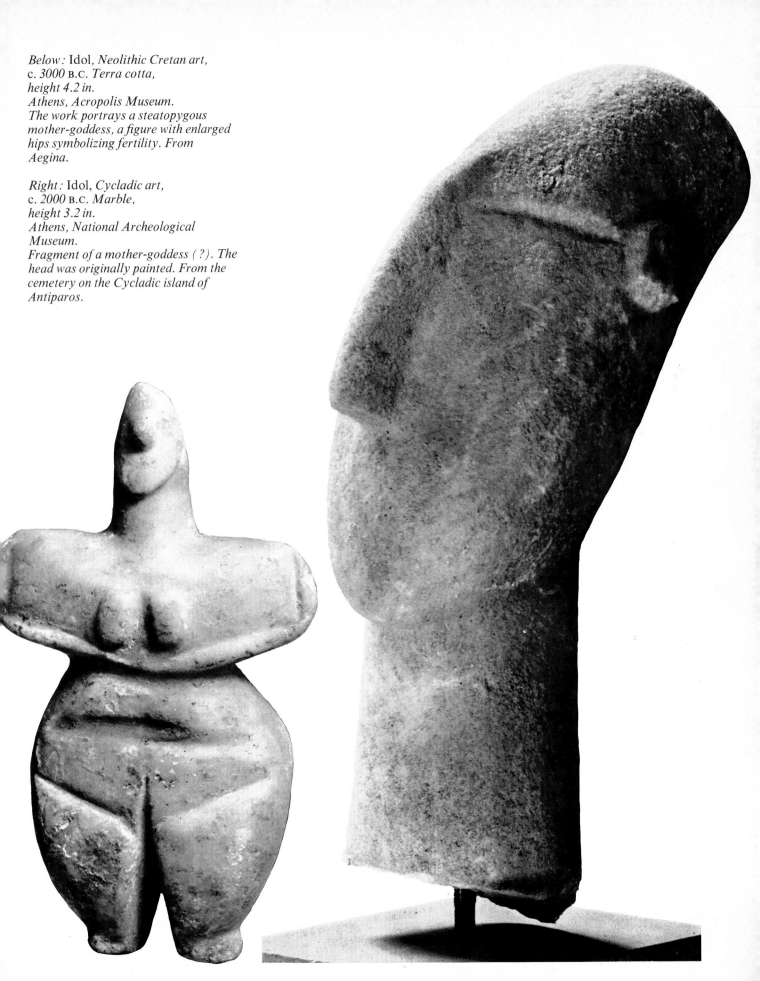

*Below:* Idol, *Neolithic Cretan art,*
*c. 3000 B.C. Terra cotta,*
*height 4.2 in.*
*Athens, Acropolis Museum.*
*The work portrays a steatopygous*
*mother-goddess, a figure with enlarged*
*hips symbolizing fertility. From*
*Aegina.*

*Right:* Idol, *Cycladic art,*
*c. 2000 B.C. Marble,*
*height 3.2 in.*
*Athens, National Archeological*
*Museum.*
*Fragment of a mother-goddess (?). The*
*head was originally painted. From the*
*cemetery on the Cycladic island of*
*Antiparos.*

81

*Left:* Female Goddess, *Cretan art (Late Minoan III), 1400–1200* B.C. *Terra cotta, height 20.7 in. Heraklion, Museum. The unknown goddess is shown with her arms raised in a ritual position; her crown is decorated with doves, birds that were later sacred to Aphrodite. A type of statuette that was possibly intended for domestic worship. From Gazi, near Heraklion.*

*Page 33:* Ithyphallic Idol, *Neolithic Thessalonian art, 2500–2200* B.C. *Terra cotta, height 18.9 in. Athens, National Archeological Museum. The male divinity with exaggerated genital organs was a symbol of fertility throughout the Mediterranean area. From Thessaly.*

*Page 35:* Bull's-Head Rhyton, *Cretan art (Late Minoan I),* c. *1500* B.C. *Carved steatite, inlaid nostrils (shell) and eyes (rock crystal), height 14 in. Heraklion, Museum. The rhyton, a vessel intended for ritual libations, originated in the East; the bull's-head form was very common in Crete (the bull was the sacred animal of the island). This example has a lid over the neck and there is a hole in the head for pouring the wine. The original horns were covered in gold plate. From the Little Palace of Knossos.*

*Right:* Cup, *Cretan art (Late Minoan I),* c. *1500* B.C. *Bas-relief, steatite, height 4.5 in. Heraklion, Museum. Conical votive goblet decorated with figures of armed warriors. From Hagia Triada in the eastern part of Crete.*

*Left:* Idol, *Cretan art
(Late Minoan I),* c. *1500* B.C.
*Bronze, height 9 in.
Athens, National Archeological
Museum.
The statuette portrays a young man
wearing a loincloth. His right hand is
resting on his forehead in a gesture of
worship before a deity.*

*Pages 36 and 37:* Lion Gate,
*Mycenaean art,* c. *1300* B.C. *High relief,
limestone, height 9.8 ft.
width at base 9.8 ft.
Mycenae. The triangular block stands
high above a gate in the cyclopean walls
of Mycenae. Two lions are portrayed in
profile, heads facing the front and
forelegs resting on a plinth supporting
the central column. Their meaning is
obscure. They could be magico-
religious symbols or they could indicate
the power of the ruling family
(throughout Asia and the
Mediterranean the lion was the symbol
of royalty).*

*Page 38:* Gold Mask, *Mycenaean art,*
c. *1500* B.C. *Embossed gold,
height 11.9 in.
Athens, National Archeological
Museum.
The mask portrays a man's face with a
mustache and beard. According to
Mycenaean burial practice a mask was
placed over the corpse's face. (This
mask was found by Heinrich
Schliemann in Grave IV at Mycenae in
1876.)*

*Right:* Snake Goddess, *Cretan art
(Late Minoan I),* c. *1500* B.C.
*Faience, height 11.6 in.
Heraklion, Museum.
The work portrays the Mediterranean
mother-goddess of fertility in one of the
guises she assumed when she appeared
before mortals. In her hands are snakes
(the symbol of life) and on her head is
a lion, her animal escort. According to
another interpretation, this is a votive
statuette, portraying a princess in court
dress, performing the ritual functions of
the goddess's priestess. From the
Palace of Knossos.*

*Above and page 87, top:* Vaphio Cup,
*Cretan art (Late Minoan I).*
*c. 1500 B.C.*
*Embossed gold, height 3.1 in.*
*Athens, National Archeological
Museum.*
*The cup depicts a bull caught in a net
(top, left), a wild bull (top, right),
and a bull trying to escape, knocking
one man down while another holds the
animal by the left horn (p. 87). It was
made in Crete, but found in a grave at
Vaphio in southern Laconia.*

*Left and page 87, bottom:* Vaphio Cup
*Cretan art (Late Minoan I),*
*c. 1500 B.C. Embossed gold,*
*height 3.3 in.*
*Athens, National Archeological
Museum.*
*On this cup, similar to the one above,
with which it was found, are portrayed
a bull and a heifer (on the left), a wild
bull (on the left, bottom), and a man
tying the hind legs of a captured bull
(on p. 87).*

*Above:* Perseus and the Gorgon, *Archaic art,*
*early 7th century* B.C.
*Bas-relief, ivory, 3.9 × 3.9 in.*
*Samos, Archeological Museum.*
*The fragment, from the Temple of Hera at Samos,*
*portrays the Attic hero cutting off the head of Medusa, one*
*of the three Gorgons (he will afterwards give it to Athena,*
*behind him, who will put it on her shield). The monster,*
*whose glance and voice turned men to stone, is portrayed*
*according to Mesopotamian iconography in which the hero*
*Khumbaba kills a similar monster in the saga of*
*Gilgamesh.*

*Right:* Aristocles, Stele of Aristion *(detail), Archaic art,*
*c. 510–500* B.C. *Bas-relief, marble with traces of colour,*
*height 79.6 in., width at base 16.2 in. Athens, National*
*Archeological Museum. The gravestone depicts Aristion*
*dressed as a warrior, with helmet, cuirass, greaves, and a*
*spear in his left hand. The bearded face is framed in short*
*hair combed into ringlets. The inscription on the base gives*
*the name of the deceased and the sculptor. From*
*Velanidesa in Attica.*

*Page 90, left:* Tyskiewicz Apollo, *Archaic art,*
*c. 700–680* B.C. *Bronze, height 7.9 in.*
*Boston, Museum of Fine Arts.*
*According to the inscription on the thighs, the mutilated*
*statuette depicts Apollo and was dedicated to the god by a*
*man named Mantiklos. The god is naked and is wearing a*
*helmet over long hair combed into ringlets. From Boeotia,*
*formerly in the Tyskiewicz Collection.*


*Page 90, right:* Hermes, *Archaic art,*
*c. 510–500* B.C. *Bronze, height 9.9 in.*
*Boston, Museum of Fine Arts.*
*The votive statuette depicts Hermes in his capacity as*
*protector of flocks, which is indicated by the ram he is*
*holding in his left arm. The winged boots are the god's*
*attributes, as are the short traveller's tunic tied at the*
*waist, the special hat, and the stick in his right hand (lost).*
*The work was probably made in a Sicyon workshop.*


*Right:* Artemis *or* Nikandra of Delos, *Cretan art from*
*the "orientalizing" period, second half of the*
*7th century* B.C. *Marble, height 74.9 in.*
*Athens, National Archeological Museum.*
*The goddess is dressed in a straight garment tied at the*
*waist and wears her unbound hair in ringlets over her*
*shoulders. The inscription at the bottom on the left*
*indicates that it is a votive statue, dedicated to the goddess*
*by a Naxian woman called Nikandra. Found at Delos in*
*front of the Temple of Apollo (Apollo was the twin brother*
*of Artemis).*

*Left:* Auxerre Goddess, *Cretan art from the "orientalizing" period, second half of the 7th century* B.C. *Limestone, height 29.6 in. Paris, Louvre.*
*The work is traditionally known by the name of the French city in whose museum it stood before being exhibited at the Louvre. A votive statuette to an unknown deity, it depicts a woman dressed in a straight tunic decorated with a geometric meander motif engraved on the stone. A short, heavy cape is draped over her shoulders; her hair is combed into long ringlets.*

*Page 39:* Dipylon Head, *Archaic art, c. 610–600* B.C. *Athens, National Archeological Museum.*
*The head, framed by curls held in a band, is probably a fragment from a nude statue of a whole figure. From the Athenian cemetery that lay beyond the Dipylon gate on the northwestern side of the walls during the Archaic period.*

*Page 47:* Amazonomachy, *Archaic art, second half of the 6th century* B.C. *Embossed silver and pale gold, height 8.5 in. London, British Museum.*
*The sheet depicts a battle between Greeks and Amazons, or between Greeks and Scythian archers. Almost certainly intended to decorate a chariot, it was found in Castel San Mariano near Perugia, together with other similar pieces made of bronze or silver. Their origin is disputed. They were either imported from Clazomenae in Ionia or, more probably, they were produced on Etruscan soil where craftsmanship in the sixth century showed considerable Ionian influence (decorated chariots were typical of Italy, however). Other articles found indicate that the Perugia region was the home of skilled metalworkers.*

*Right:* Achilles (and Penthesilea?), *Archaic art, c. 600* B.C. *Terra cotta bas-relief, height 16.5 in. New York, Metropolitan Museum of Art.*
*The gravestone, in Attic style, depicts the hero fighting during the Trojan war (possibly with Penthesilea, the queen of the Amazons). Achilles, naked, is grasping a spear and is wearing a protective Corinthian helmet and carrying a shield decorated with the head of Medusa.*

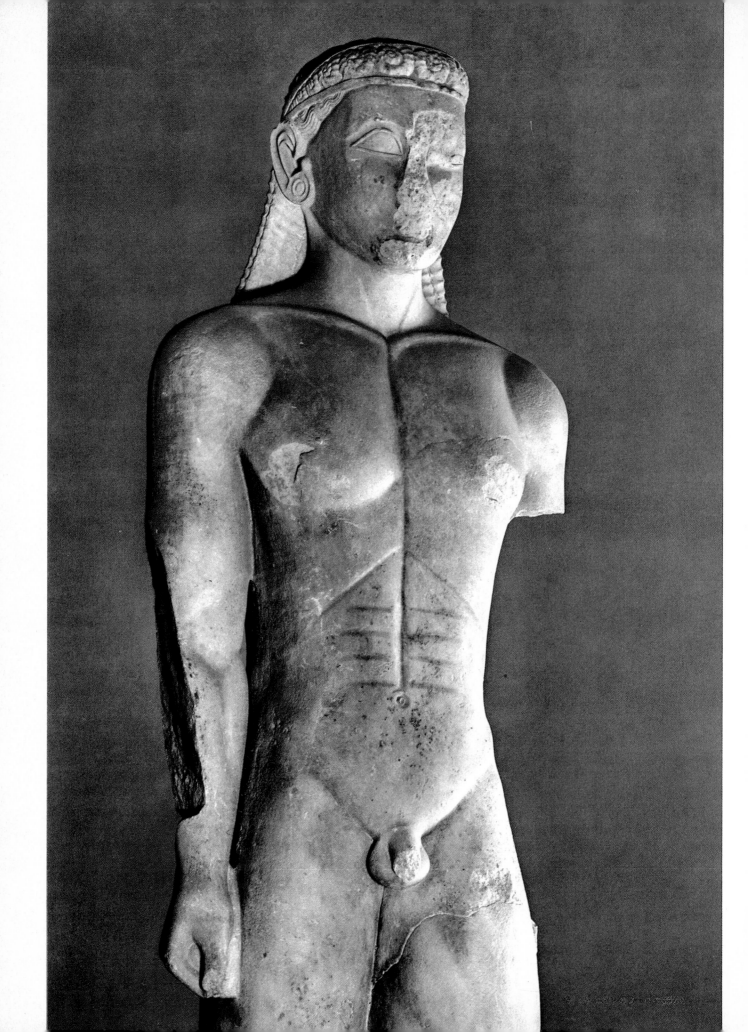

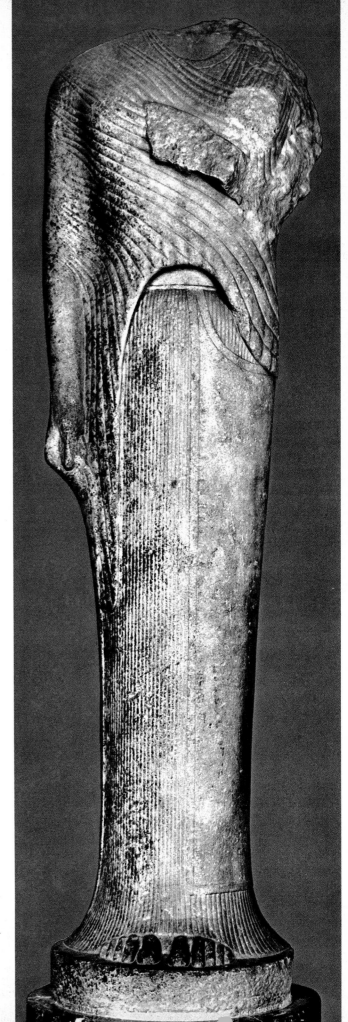

*Left:* Sunium Kouros *(detail). Archaic art,*
c. *610–600* B.C. *Marble, height 9.8 in.*
*Athens, National Archeological Museum.*
*The* kouros *("youth" in Greek) type of sculpture depicts the naked youthful figure of a votary who has dedicated a statue of himself to a deity. This example, the oldest that has survived intact, shows the characteristic stance—arms down at the sides, fists clenched, the left leg stretched forward to improve the statue's balance. The curls on the forehead are held in a band, and the rest of the hair is arranged down the back in long braids. From the Temple of Poseidon at Cape Sunium in Attica.*

*Page 40:* Three-bodied Monster from the Hekatompedon,
*Archaic art,* c. *560–550* B.C. *Painted limestone, height 27.8 in.*
*Athens, National Archeological Museum.*
*The illustration shows one of the bearded male faces (first from the right) of the three-bodied monster that occupied the right side of the Hekatompedon pediment. The monster, whose body ends in a snake's tail, is shown taking part in the fight between Heracles and Triton (on the left). The Hekatompedon ("hundred feet long") was an Archaic temple on the Athens Acropolis.*

*Page 41:* Ronbos, Moschophorus *(detail), Archaic art,* c. *570–560* B.C. *Hymettian marble, total height 65 in., height from the knees 37.8 in. (legs restored).*
*Athens, National Archeological Museum.*
*The statue portrays a calf bearer offering a victim for sacrifice. Originally the beard was painted and the eyes were inlaid with onyx. The chiton (tunic-like garment) is transparent, and is emphasized by raised vertical lines indicating the seams. The sculptor's name is given in the inscription engraved on the base. From the Athens Acropolis.*

*Right:* Hera of Samos, *Archaic art,*
c. *560* B.C. *Marble, height 76.8 in.*
*Paris, Louvre.*
*The headless, column-shaped female figure is dressed in a chiton and himation (pleated tunic and short cape) with a straight veil down her back. The inscription on the base indicates that it is a statue of Hera, dedicated to the goddess by a man called Cheramyes. From the Temple of Hera at Samos.*

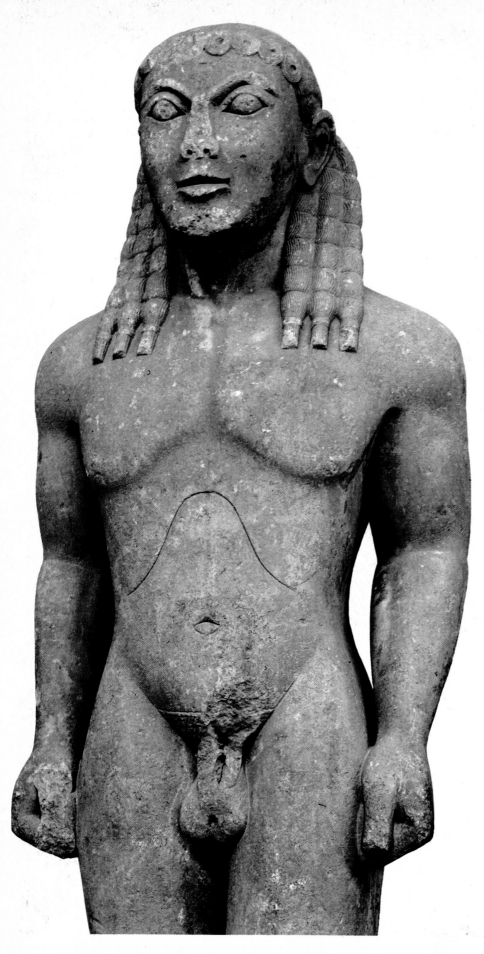

Left: Biton (detail), Archaic art,
c. 590–580 B.C. Parian marble,
height 85.9 in.
Delphi, Museum.
The statue is one of two depicting
Cleobis and Biton, the twin sons of the
priestess Cydippe. According to legend
they pulled their mother's coach to
Hera's sanctuary and when Cydippe
begged the gods to give her sons their
most precious gift, Hera made them fall
into everlasting sleep.

Page 42: Anavysos Kouros,
Archaic art,
c. 530–520 B.C. Marble,
height 76.4 in.
Athens, National Archeological
Museum.
According to the inscription engraved
on the base, the kouros was made in
memory of a man called Croesus who
had been killed in battle. From
Anavysos in southern Attica.

Page 97, left: Tenea Apollo
(in profile), Archaic art,
c. 560–550 B.C. Marble,
height 60.3 in.
Munich, Glyptothek.
Despite its name, the statue depicts a
kouros (a statue of a devout youth
dedicated to a deity), with long wavy
hair falling loose over his shoulders.
From Tenea near Corinth.

Page 97, right: Kouros,
Archaic art, c. 550–540 B.C.
Marble, height 83 in.
Munich, Glyptothek.
This kouros, of Attic type, is
characterized by his powerful shoulder
and thigh muscles and by his short curly
hair fastened in a band.

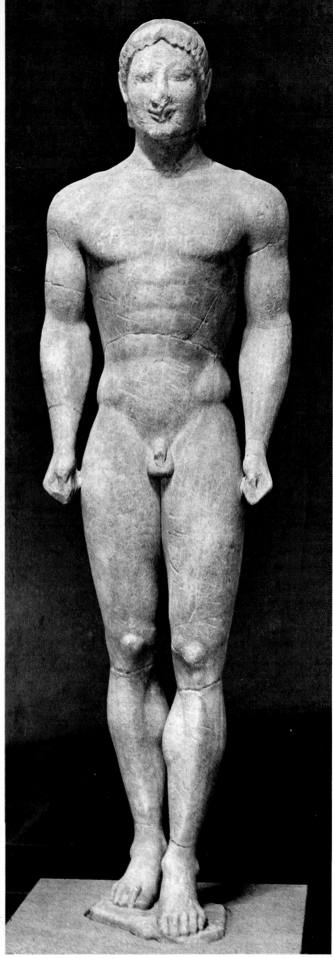

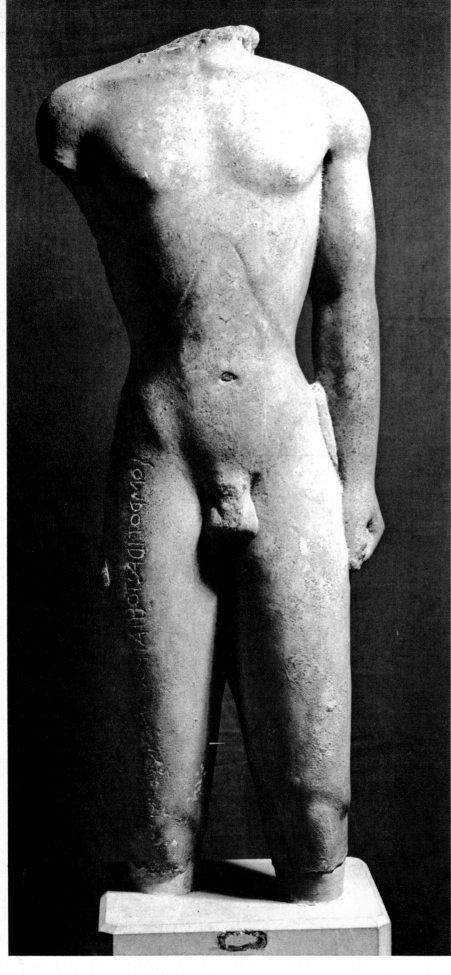

*Left:* Kouros, *Archaic art,*
*c. 550–540* B.C. *Marble,*
*height 46.9 in.*
*Syracuse, Archeological Museum.*
*This mutilated statue, dedicated by the*
*physician Sombrotides, comes from*
*Megara Hyblaea in Sicily.*

*Above:* Gigantomachy *(detail),*
*Siphnian*
*Treasury at Delphi. Archaic art,*
*c. 525* B.C. *Relief, marble,*
*height 25.2 in.*
*Delphi, Museum.*
*The work formed the north frieze of the*
*treasury (small votive temple)*
*dedicated in the Delphi sanctuary by*
*the inhabitants of the Cycladic island of*
*Siphnos.*

*Right:* Horses Pulling a Chariot and
Riders *(detail), from the Siphnian*
*Treasury at Delphi, Archaic art,*
*c. 525* B.C. *Relief, marble,*
*height 25.2 in.*
*Delphi, Museum.*
*The frieze depicts Castor and*
*Polydeuces (Pollux is his Latin name)*
*carrying off the daughters of*
*Leucippus, the king of Messenia.*

*Top:* Quadriga and Homeric Heroes *(detail),*
*from the Siphnian Treasury at Delphi,*
*Archaic art,* c. 525 B.C.
*Relief, marble, height 25.2 in.*
*East frieze (right side) of the Siphnian*
*Treasury (see caption on p. 98),*
*depicting Trojans and Acheans fighting*
*in the presence of the gods.*

*Above:* Assembled Gods *(detail),*
*from the Siphnian Treasury at Delphi.*
*Archaic art,* c. 525 B.C.
*Relief, marble, height 25.2 in.*
*Delphi, Museum.*
*East frieze (left side) of the Siphnian*
*Treasury (see caption on p. 98),*
*depicting, from the left, Ares, three*
*goddesses, and Zeus watching the*
*battle between the Trojans and*
*Acheans.*

*Right:* Gigantomachy *(detail),*
*Siphnian Treasury at Delphi,*
*Archaic art,* c. 525 B.C.
*Relief, marble, height 25.2 in.*
*Delphi, Museum.*
*Detail from the northern frieze of the*
*Siphnian Treasury (illustration on pp.*
*98–99, top) showing Ares, the god of*
*war, fighting (on the left).*

100

*Left (back and front views) and right (detail of profile):*
Goddess with a Pomegranate,
*Archaic art, c. 580–570* B.C.
*Painted marble, height 76 in.*
*Berlin, Staatliche Museen.*
*The statue depicts a woman or an unknown goddess holding a pomegranate, the symbol of the renewal of life, in her right hand. The garment with long pleats and short cape is of Corinthian type; the feet are shod in sandals, which is unusual. On the wavy hair, held in a band and gathered into a tail on the back, is the* polos, *a cylindrical headdress. The neck is adorned with a choker with pendants and around the wrist is a spiral bracelet.*

*Pages 44 and 45:* Gigantomachy *(detail),*
*from the Siphnian Treasury at Delphi,*
*Archaic art,* c. *525* B.C.
*Relief, marble, height 25.2 in.*
*Delphi, Museum.*
*Detail from the northern frieze of the Siphnian Treasury (see caption on p. 98), depicting one of the giants trying to scale Olympus. The lion on the left is one of the animals fighting on the side of the gods.*

103

*Above:* Two Lions Devouring a Bull,
*Archaic art, 6th century* B.C. *High relief, limestone,
height 38.2 in., length 16 ft.
Athens, Acropolis Museum.
The group depicted a dead bull and two attacking lions
(only the bull's legs are left). It was found on the Athens
Acropolis, where it decorated an altar or a pediment.*

*Right:* Lioness Devouring a Bull, *Archaic art,
6th century* B.C. *High relief, limestone,
height 6.3 in., length 9.8 ft.
Athens, Acropolis Museum.
The group was found in fragments on the Athens
Acropolis, where it probably formed one half of a
pediment.*

*Above:* Stele of a Discophorus, *Archaic art,* c. 560–550 B.C. *Bas-relief, Pentelic marble, height 15 in. Athens, National Archeological Museum. Fragment of a gravestone depicting a discus thrower. The athlete was almost certainly represented standing in profile, with the discus in his left hand (a fragment of thumb is still visible above his shoulder), balancing his instrument before spinning into the throw. From the Athens cemetery outside the Dipylon gate.*

*Right:* Rampin Horseman, *the head, Archaic art,* c. 560 B.C. *Painted marble, height 10.6 in. Paris, Louvre. The man's head (which takes its name from the collector who owned it) is characterized by the tiny curls of his beard and fringe. The rest of his hair is held in a narrow band and falls down the neck in thick braids. The head is now in the Louvre, but was originally part of the equestrian statue in the Athens Acropolis Museum, which indicates that the figure portrayed was an Athenian nobleman living at the time of the Peisistratids.*

*Above:* Hera, *Archaic art, c. 600–580* B.C. *Limestone, height 20.5 in. Olympia, Museum. Fragment of a lost statue found in the Temple of Hera at Olympia, possibly the work of a Spartan sculptor. It portrays a female head wearing a* polos *(a cylindrical headdress). The goddess has not been definitely identified. It has been suggested that it could be the head of a sphinx.*

*Above:* Man's Head, *Archaic art, c. 530 B.C. Marble, height 8.3 in. Paris, Louvre. A fragment of a lost statue depicting the smiling face of a mature man, with short hair, beard, and a mustache. In this period these features are also present in Attic representations of the god Dionysius.*

*Left:* Seated Goddess,
*Archaic art,* c. 480 B.C.
*Terra cotta, height 38 in.*
*Syracuse, Archeological Museum.*
*The work depicts an unknown goddess
sitting on a throne whose legs are
shaped like a lion's paws. The deity is
wearing an Ionic chiton (a tunic with
wide pleats) and a himation (a cloak
covering the shoulders). It is probably
the work of a Sicilian craftsman,
faithfully copying the Greek marble
statues that were so common in Magna
Graecia. From an unknown sanctuary
near Grammichele in Italy.*

*Page 48:* Athena Worshiped by a
Family
*(detail), Archaic art,* c. 500 B.C. *Bas-
relief,*
*marble, height 26.2 in.*
*Athens, Acropolis Museum.*
*The votive bas-relief depicts Athena
with her right knee raised and her left
hand lifting the chiton (pleated tunic)
in a ritual stance. She is wearing a
helmet. The boy standing in front of her
is offering her a sow in sacrifice. From
the Athens Acropolis.*

*Page 49:* Piombino Apollo *(detail),
Archaic art,* c. 500–490 B.C. *Bronze,
inlaid copper (eyebrows, lips, and
nipples),*
*height 45.3 in.*
*Paris, Louvre.*
*The statue has been identified as Apollo
by the position of the left hand (not
visible in the illustration) which
grasped a bow (missing). The hair,
combed into symmetrical curls, is
bound in a hairnet (a* krobylos*) on the
nape of the neck; the eyes were
originally inlaid with white enamel and
onyx. The work was found in the sea off
Piombino in 1838.*

*Right:* Fragment of a Throned Deity,
*Archaic art,* c. 530–520 B.C.
*Painted marble,
height 27.4 in.
Athens, Acropolis Museum.
The work portrays a figure on a throne,
possibly a female deity, wearing a
chiton (tunic-like garment) and a cloak
falling over the knees. Found on the
Athens Acropolis.*

*Above:* Ball Game, *Archaic art,*
c. *510* B.C. *Bas-relief, marble with
traces of colour,
height 12.6 in.,
length at base 31.9 in.
Athens, National Archeological
Museum.
The bas-relief decorated one of the
sides of a rectangular base carrying a
kouros statue and was found near
Athens's Themistoclean wall. It depicts
six youths divided into two teams
engrossed in a ball game. The young
men's hair shows traces of red colour.*

*Right:* Resting Youths, *Archaic art,*
c. *510* B.C. *Bas-relief, marble
with traces of colour,
height 12.6 in.,
length at base 31.9 in.
Athens, National Archeological
Museum.
Another side of the statue base with the
ball-game relief, it portrays two resting
athletes amusing themselves by setting
a dog on a cat; two youths behind them
are looking on.*

*Above:* Wrestlers *(detail), Archaic art,* c. *510* B.C.
*Bas-relief, marble with traces of colour,*
*height 12.6 in., length at base 31.9 in.*
*Athens, National Archeological Museum.*
*Another side of the statue base with the reliefs illustrated*
*on pp. 112 and 113. In the middle are two youths fighting;*
*the youth on the left is getting ready for a race. The three*
*reliefs portray common episodes in Athenian gymnasiums*
*at the time of the Peisistratids.*

*Right:* Abduction of Antiope *(detail), Archaic art,*
c. *510* B.C.
*Marble, height 43.3 in.*
*Chalcis, Museum.*
*The group depicts Theseus, the greatest Attic hero (on the*
*left), carrying off Antiope, the queen of the Amazons. It*
*formed part of the west pediment of the Temple of Apollo*
*Daphnephoros ("wearer of laurel") at Eretria on the*
*island of Euboea.*

*Left:* Female Dancers, *Archaic art,
c. 510–505* B.C. *Relief, marble,
height 33.5 in.,
length at base 28.2 in.
Paestum, New Archeological Museum.
The two girls, wearing chitons (pleated
tunics), their hair held in diadems, are
performing a sacred dance. Metope
from the Temple of Hera at the mouth
of the Sele (Silarus).*

*Page 43:* Kore No. 679 *or*
Peplos Kore *(detail),
Archaic art, c. 540* B.C. *Painted marble,
height 47.3 in.
Athens, Acropolis Museum.
The* kore *(see the following caption) is
wearing a peplos (a straight tunic tied
at the waist); her hair, combed into
long ringlets, is tied in a ribbon on the
nape of her neck.*

*Right:* Kore No. 674 *(detail),
Archaic art, c. 510–500* B.C.
*Painted marble,
height (from the ankles) 36.2 in.
Athens, Acropolis Museum.
The* kore *("girl" in Greek) type of
statue is a standing and clothed female
figure, depicting a priestess of Athena
or her worshiper, who has thus
dedicated a statue of herself to the
goddess as a votive offering. The* korai,
*which were very numerous and are
therefore identified by numbers, were
found buried beneath a terrace built on
the Athens Acropolis after the battle of
Salamis in 480* B.C. *(works destroyed
by the Persians were used as infilling
for the terrace). The shoulders of the*
kore, *which is badly damaged, are
covered by a* himation *(short cloak)
with very wide pleats. The wavy hair is
held in a diadem and falls down the
breast and back in long ringlets. The
right ear has lost its large round
earring, but there is one still in the left
ear.*

117

*Left:* Critian Boy *(detail),*
*Classical art,* c. 480 B.C.
*Island marble, height 33.9 in.*
*Athens, Acropolis Museum.*
*This mutilated statue of a naked youth,*
*similar to the* kouros *type (a statue of*
*a young votary dedicated to a deity), is*
*thought almost certainly to be the work*
*of the sculptor Critius. The hair is*
*gathered into a plait wound all the way*
*around the head; the eyes were*
*originally inlaid. From the Athens*
*Acropolis.*

*Page 52:* Cape Artemisium Poseidon
*(detail),*
*Classical art,* c. 460 B.C. *Bronze,*
*height 82.3 in.*
*Athens, National Archeological*
*Museum.*
*The work depicts the god of the sea*
*throwing his trident (or possibly Zeus*
*hurling a thunderbolt, as has sometimes*
*been suggested, even though the gesture*
*would have been different). The hair is*
*gathered into a plait wound around the*
*head; the eyes were originally inlaid.*
*The statue, which is possibly an*
*original by Calamis, was found in two*
*pieces between 1926 and 1928 in the sea*
*off Cape Artemisium (the northern tip*
*of the island of Euboea), where rites*
*dedicated to the cult of Poseidon took*
*place.*

*Right (whole) and page 53 (detail):*
Delphi Charioteer, *Classical art,*
*474 B.C.*
*Bronze, inlaid eyes (onyx),*
*height 70.9 in.*
*Delphi, Museum.*
*The statue formed part of a group*
*depicting a quadriga, which, according*
*to some sources, had been dedicated to*
*the Delphi Apollo by the winner of a*
*competition in the Panhellenic games.*
*The charioteer is wearing a* xystis, *a*
*long tunic tied at the waist, which was*
*worn during competitions; his right*
*hand is grasping the reins and his short*
*curls (finished with a burin) are held in*
*a band decorated with geometric motifs*
*of meanders and Greek crosses*
*(originally damascened in silver). The*
*inscription on the base indicates that*
*the quadriga was dedicated in 474 B.C.*
*by Polyzalos, the ruler of Gela.*

*Above:* Weighing of Souls, *Classical art,*
c. 470–450 B.C., *or Roman art of the 1st century* B.C.,
*or a modern fake. Relief, marble,*
*height 22 in., length at base 38 in.*
*Boston, Museum of Fine Arts.*
*Central panel of the* Boston Throne *(possibly a sacred*
*enclosure or part of an altar rather than a throne). It*
*depicts Thanatos, the god of death, as a naked, winged boy*
*weighing the dead person's life on a balance (missing).*
*The two female figures seated on cushions on each side are*
*symbols of the two natures (joy and melancholy) of the*
*dead person's soul. The authenticity of the work has been*
*seriously questioned. However, some scholars do not*
*regard it as a modern fake. They believe it is an original*
*dating from the age of Imperial Rome (1st century* B.C.),
*which was produced as a "companion" to the* Ludovisi
Throne *(right). Its provenance from the ancient Gardens*
*of Sallust in Rome has not been established.*

*Page 54:* Lyre Player. *Relief, marble,*
*height 18.9 in.*
*Boston, Museum of Fine Arts.*
*Side panel of the* Boston Throne, *showing a naked youth*
*sitting on a cushion playing funerary melodies on a lyre.*

*Right and page 55 (details):*
Birth of Aphrodite, *Classical art,* c. 470–450 B.C.
*Relief, marble, height 40.9 in.,*
*length at base 56.7 in.*
*Rome, National Museum of the Terme.*
*Central panel of the* Ludovisi Throne *(more probably*
*part of an altar or an enclosure for ritual sacrifices). The*
*traditional identification of the scene is open to doubt;*
*besides depicting the birth of the goddess emerging from*
*the sea spray with the aid of two handmaidens, it could*
*also be a representation of a ritual (sacred immersion?)*
*connected with the cult of Persephone. Found in Rome in*
*1887 in the garden of the Villa Ludovisi, near the Gardens*
*of Sallust.*

*Above and right (details);* Dying Warrior,
*from the Temple of Athena Aphaea at Aegina, Archaic
art,* c. *500–480* B.C.
*Marble, height 18.5 in., length 62.6 in.
Munich, Glyptothek.
The figure occupied the right corner of the west pediment
in the Temple of Athena Aphaea at Aegina. On the
pediment were depicted two episodes from the Trojan war
on either side of a statue of Athena (the two groups
portrayed Ajax and Teucer and Aeneas and Paris fighting
for possession of Achilles' body). The work's present
scoured surface is the result of restoration in the 19th
century by the neoclassical sculptor Thorvaldsen.*

*Page 46:* Dying Warrior *(detail),
from the Temple of Athena Aphaea at Aegina,
Archaic art,* c. *500–480* B.C.
*Marble, height 25.2 in., length 72.9 in.
Munich, Glyptothek.
This naked warrior, with helmet and shield, was positioned
in the left corner of the east pediment of the Temple of
Athena Aphaea at Aegina, which depicted the battle
between Heracles and Laomedon.*

122

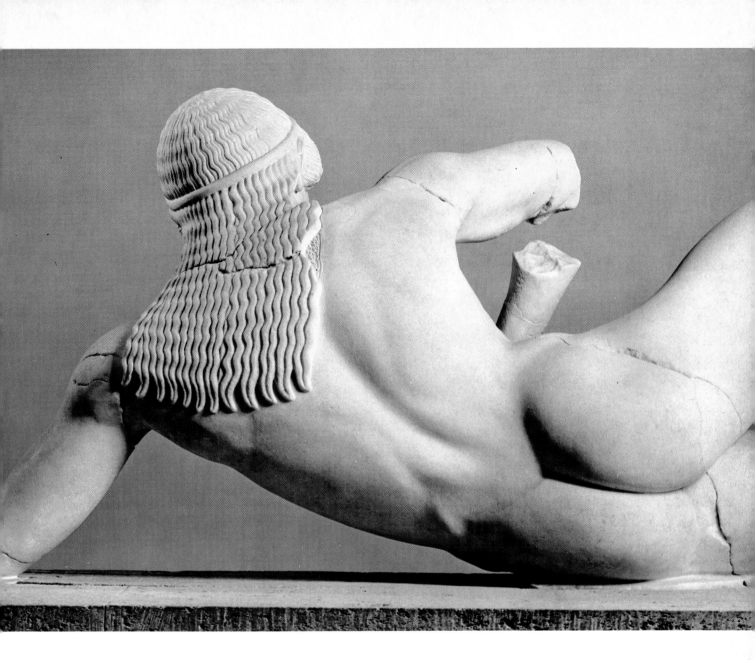

*Above:* Theseus,
*from the Temple of Zeus at Olympia,*
*Classical art, c. 470–456 B.C.*
*Parian marble, height 13.8 in.*
*Olympia, Museum.*
*Fragment of a statue of Theseus that stood in the*
*west pediment of the Temple of Zeus at Olympia.*
*Theseus, a friend of Pelops, was helping to fight*
*the centaurs who wanted to carry off the Lapith*
*women and children (see caption on p. 127).*

*On the right:* Heracles, *from the Temple of*
*Athena Aphaea at Aegina, Archaic art,*
*c. 500–480 B.C. Marble, height 31 in.*
*Munich, Glyptothek.*
*The hero, wearing armour, is shown on his knees, drawing*
*his bow (the arrow, missing, was almost certainly of*
*metal). The statue stood in the east pediment of the*
*Temple of Athena Aphaea at Aegina, which depicted*
*Heracles and Laomedon, watched by Athena, fighting for*
*possession of Ajax's body during the Trojan war.*

Left and page 50 (details):
Lapith Woman and Centaur, from
the Temple of Zeus at Olympia,
Classical art, c. 470–456 B.C.
Parian marble,
height about 98 in.
Olympia, Museum. The group portrays
a Lapith woman trying to escape from
a centaur who wants to carry her off. A
detail from the west pediment of the
Temple of Zeus at Olympia, depicting
the battle between the Lapiths and
centaurs. The centaurs, creatures with
a human torso on the body of a horse,
were the sons of Apollo, and had been
invited to the wedding of Pelops and
Hippodamia, daughter of the king of
the Lapiths. They became drunk and
tried to carry off the guests' women and
children, but were defeated in the
ensuing battle. To the Greeks the myth
of the Centauromachy, which was often
depicted on metopes and pediments,
symbolized the victory of civilization
over brute force.

Page 51: Zeus Carrying Off
Ganymede,
Classical art, c. 470 B.C.
Painted terra cotta, height 43.3 in.
Olympia, Museum.
The work portrays the legendary story
of Zeus (dressed as a traveller with a
staff in his left hand), who is so
attracted by the beauty of the shepherd
boy Ganymede, the future cup bearer of
the gods, that he carries him off. It is
almost certainly an acroterium (a
figurative group that was put at the
ends or at the apex of a pediment),
which originally stood on one of the
many small votive temples around the
Temple of Zeus at Olympia.

Right; Apollo (detail),
from the Temple of Zeus at Olympia,
Classical art, c. 470–456 B.C.
Parian marble, height 9.8 ft.
Olympia, Museum.
The central figure on the west pediment
of the Temple of Zeus at Olympia,
depicting Apollo presiding over the
battle between the Lapiths and centaurs
(see caption above).

*Above:* Death of Actaeon *(detail), from Temple E at Selinus, Classical art,* c. 460–450 B.C. *Relief, limestone and marble with traces of colour, height 63.8 in., length at base 55 in. Palermo, National Museum. Metope of Temple E at Selinus, dedicated to Hera. The work portrays the myth of the hunter-prince Actaeon (shown naked, with an animal skin over his shoulders) who is turned into a stag by Artemis (fragments of the horns are visible on the slab) and as a result torn to pieces by his own dogs.*

*Above and page 2 (details):* Marriage of Hera and Zeus, *from Temple E at Selinus, Classical art,* c. *460–450* B.C. *Relief, limestone and marble with traces of colour, height 63.8 in., length at base 55 in. Palermo, National Museum. Metope of Temple E at Selinus, dedicated to Hera. The work portrays Zeus removing Hera's veil and uncovering her face.*

*Left:* Stele of Athena,
*Classical art,* c. *460* B.C.
*Bas-relief, marble,*
*height 24.4 in.*
*Athens, Acropolis Museum.*
*The work portrays Athena, wearing a*
*battle helmet and a peplos (a pleated*
*garment fastened on the shoulders and*
*tied at the waist), of the Classical*
*period, leaning thoughtfully on her*
*spear in front of a gravestone.*
*According to another interpretation,*
*Athena is standing in front of a*
*boundary pillar, and this ties in with the*
*fact that she was also the goddess of*
*boundaries. If this is the case, the work*
*could be a votive stele from the wall*
*around the Athens Acropolis (built by*
*Cimon between 470 and 460* B.C.*).*
*From the Athens Acropolis.*

*Right:* Great Eleusinian Relief *or*
Triptolemus between Demeter and
Kore, *Classical art,* c. *450* B.C.
*Relief, marble, height 25.6 in.*
*Athens, National Archeological*
*Museum. The work portrays the*
*concluding episode in the Eleusinian*
*Mysteries, which were connected with*
*the cult of Demeter, the goddess of*
*agriculture and fertility. While looking*
*for her daughter Persephone (or*
*Kore), who has been abducted by*
*Hades, the god of the underworld,*
*Demeter is shown hospitality by*
*Celeus, the king of Eleusis. She*
*rewards him by giving his son*
*Triptolemus a chariot driven by winged*
*dragons and some ears of corn so that*
*he can bring agriculture to mankind.*
*The relief shows the young Triptolemus*
*standing between Demeter (on the*
*left), who is giving him the ears of corn,*
*and Persephone (on the right), who is*
*holding a torch and crowning him. The*
*relief, which can be attributed to a*
*follower of Phidias, comes from Eleusis*
*and probably stood in the Telesterion,*
*the temple where initiation rites were*
*held.*

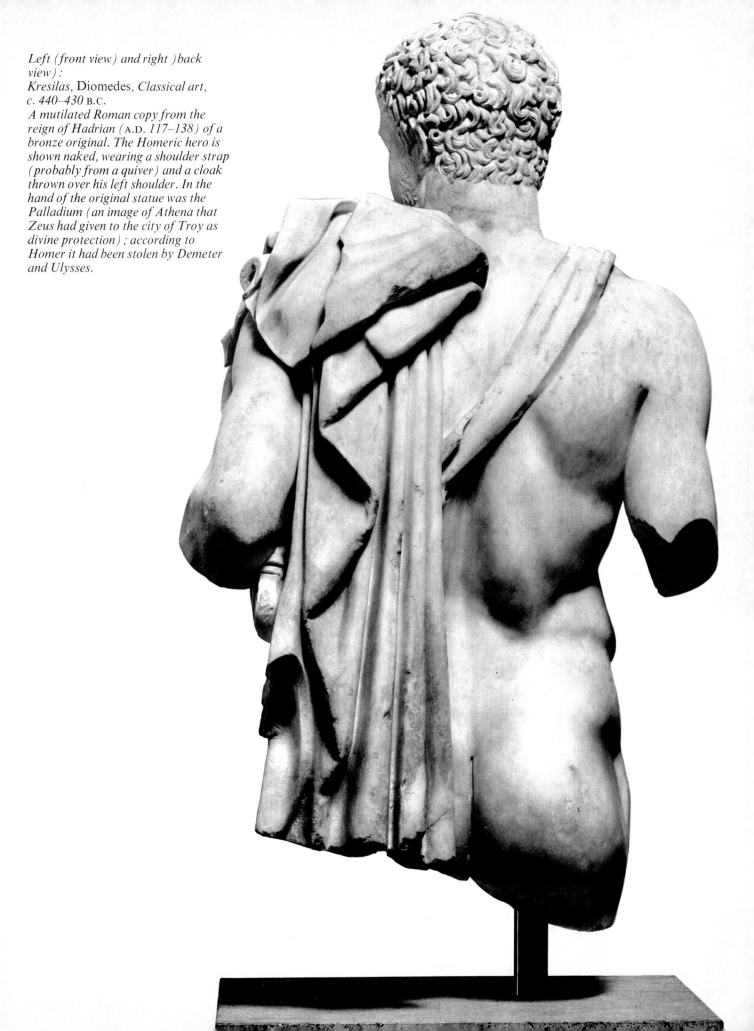

*Left (front view) and right ) back view ):*
*Kresilas, Diomedes, Classical art, c. 440–430 B.C.*
*A mutilated Roman copy from the reign of Hadrian (A.D. 117–138) of a bronze original. The Homeric hero is shown naked, wearing a shoulder strap (probably from a quiver) and a cloak thrown over his left shoulder. In the hand of the original statue was the Palladium (an image of Athena that Zeus had given to the city of Troy as divine protection); according to Homer it had been stolen by Demeter and Ulysses.*

*Above: Phidias,* Three Goddesses, *from the Parthenon, Classical art, c. 448–435 B.C. Pentelic marble, height 47.6 in. London, British Museum. The group of three goddesses, which have been identified (from the left) as Hestia, Diana, and Aphrodite, stood in the extreme right of the east pediment of the Parthenon, the temple on the Athens Acropolis dedicated to Athena Parthenos, the patroness of the city. The pediment portrays Athena's birth, springing from Zeus' head already fully grown and armed, in the presence of the Olympian gods. The central group, showing Athena, Zeus, and Hera, has been destroyed, while the west pediment (depicting the contest between Poseidon and Athena for possession of Attica) and most of the metopes and the cella frieze were seriously damaged in 1687. (The Turks had turned the temple into a powder magazine, which blew up when it was bombarded by the Venetian army besieging the city.) In the early 1800s the Phidian sculptures were taken to London by the English diplomat Lord Elgin, and in 1816 they were sold to the British government.*

*Above, Phidias,* Group of Gods, *from the Parthenon, Classical art, c. 448–435 B.C. Pentelic marble, height 11 ft., length at base about 46 ft. London, British Museum. The extreme left of the east pediment of the Parthenon (see caption on p. 134), depicting, from the left, the horses pulling the chariot of the sun god Helios out of the sea, and Dionysius, Demeter, Persephone, and Iris attending Athena's birth. According to another interpretation, the three female figures could depict the Horae.*

*Page 56:* Tiber Apollo *(detail), Classical art, c. 460 B.C. Marble, height 66 in. Rome, National Museum of the Terme. The god is portrayed naked, with his loose hair held in a band. It is possibly a copy of a bronze original by the young Phidias (depicting Miltiades standing between Apollo and Athena) dedicated in the god's sanctuary at Delphi to commemorate the battle of Marathon. The work, partially restored, was found in 1891 in the Tiber.*

*Page 138: Phidias,* Persephone
*(detail), from the Parthenon,
Classical art,* c. *448–435* B.C.
*Pentelic marble, height 58.3 in.
London, British Museum.
Detail from the east pediment of
the Parthenon.*

*Page 139: Phidias,* Dionysius
*(detail), from the Parthenon,
Classical art,* c. *448–435* B.C.
*Pentelic marble.
London, British Museum.
Detail from the east pediment of
the Parthenon.*

*Above and right: Phidias and collaborators,*
Procession of Riders *(detail),*
*from the Parthenon,*
*Classical art, c. 448–435 B.C.*
*Bas-relief, Pentelic marble,*
*height 41.7 in.*
*London, British Museum.*
*Details from the frieze, originally*
*522 ft. long, that ran around the top of*
*the four external walls of the*
*Parthenon cella. The frieze, which was*
*visible from inside the colonnade,*
*depicts the procession that went up to*
*the Acropolis during the annual*
*Panathenaic festival held in honour of*
*the goddess Athena.*

*At the head are girls of noble family*
*carrying the peplos that is to be offered*
*to the goddess; behind them winds the*
*procession of riders, musicians, and*
*bearers of sacrificial animals, followed*
*by the rest of the population.*

*Page 57: Phidias*, Athena Parthenos
*(detail),*
*Classical art*, c. *438* B.C. *(Roman copy).*
*Marble, height 37 in.*
*Athens, National Archeological Museum.*
*The most famous version, dating from the age of Imperial Rome (1st century* A.D.*), of the enormous statue of Athena that Phidias carved in gold and ivory for the cella of the Athens Parthenon. The original, now lost, was 26 ft. high,* *and has been fully described by his contemporaries. Athena is depicted as the goddess of victory and wisdom; a sphinx and two winged horses decorate her helmet. In her right hand she holds Nike—the personification of victory— and at her left side leans a shield, which on the inside is decorated with the Amazonomachy and on the outside with the Gigantomachy, symbols of the superiority of Greek civilization over barbarism and brute force.*

*Left : Phidias and collaborators*, Ergastinai
*(detail), from the Parthenon,*
*Classical art, 439–432* B.C.
*Bas-relief, Pentelic marble,*
*height 41.7 in.*
*Paris, Louvre.*
*Detail from the Parthenon frieze (see caption on p. 140),*
*depicting the Ergastinai, the girls of the Athenian nobility*
*who wove the peplos that was offered to the goddess*
*Athena during the Panathenaic festivities.*

*Above : Phidias and collaborators*, Centauromachy,
*from the Parthenon, Classical art, 447–443* B.C.
*High relief, Pentelic marble,*
*height 52.8 in., length at base 50 in.*
*London, British Museum.*
*Parthenon metope (see caption on p. 144), depicting a*
*fight between a centaur and a Lapith at the wedding of*
*Hippodamia and Pelops (see caption on p. 127).*

*Above and right (detail): Phidias and collaborators,*
Centauromachy, *from the Parthenon, Classical art,*
*447–443* B.C.
*High relief, Pentelic marble,*
*height 52.8 in.; length at base 50 in.*
*London, British Museum.*
*Two of the ninety-two metopes that decorated the four*
*sides of the Parthenon architrave. The scenes of legendary*
*battles symbolize the superiority of Hellenic civilization.*
*On the east (on the main side) was the* Gigantomachy

*(the war between the gods and giants), on the north the*
Fall of Troy, *on the west the* Amazonomachy *(the war*
*between the Amazons and the inhabitants of Attica), and*
*on the south the* Centauromachy *(between centaurs and*
Lapiths). *Only nineteen metopes have survived, several of*
*which are still on the temple; the rest are in London (see*
*caption on p. 134). Most were broken up when the temple*
*was turned into a Christian church. The destruction was*
*completed by the explosion of 1687.*

*Above and right (details):*
Amazonomachy,
*from the Mausoleum at Halicarnassus,*
*Classical art, c. 350–333 B.C.*
*Relief, marble, height 35.5 in.*
*London, British Museum.*
*Three slabs from the frieze of the*
*Mausoleum, the sepulcher that*
*Artemisia had built at Halicarnassus in*
*honour of her husband Mausolus, a*
*satrap of Caria in Asia Minor, who had*
*died in 353 B.C. The frieze portrays the*
*battle between the Amazons and the*
*inhabitants of Attica, which the*
*warrior-women had invaded to avenge*
*the abduction of their queen Antiope by*
*Theseus. Literary sources (Pliny) give*
*Bryaxis, Scopas, Timotheus, and*
*Leochares as the respective sculptors of*
*the four sides. The monument was*
*destroyed by crusaders in the 12th*
*century, and the discovered remains*
*have been variously attributed. The*
*illustrated slabs are ascribed to Scopas*
*(on the right and top left) and Bryaxis*
*(top right).*

146

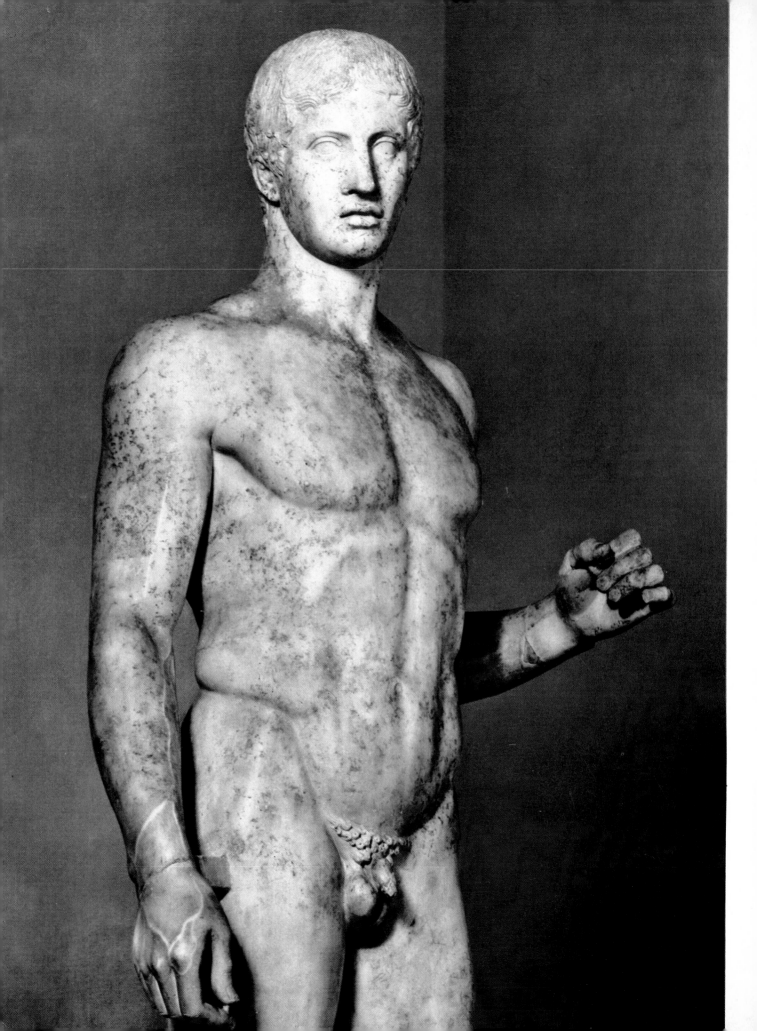

*Left (detail) and page 21: Polyclitus,* Doryphorus, *Classical art, c. 450–440* B.C. *(Roman copy).*
*Marble, height 83.5 in.*
*Naples, National Archeological Museum.*
*The Polyclitus original was made of bronze. The work, depicting a spear bearer with his weapon balanced over the left shoulder, probably represents the hero Achilles. From the Samnite palaestra at Pompeii.*

*Above: Phidias,* Laborde Head, *Classical art, 439–432* B.C.
*Marble, height 15.8 in. Paris, Louvre.*
*Fragment of a female statue, possibly representing Nike, the goddess of victory. From the west pediment of the Parthenon. The name it is traditionally known by comes from the Marquis Léon de Laborde, who acquired the work in Venice during the 17th century.*

*Left:* Stele of Hegeso, *Classical art,* c. 410–400 B.C.
*Bas-relief, marble, height 62.2 in., length at base 39.5 in.*
*Athens, National Archeological Museum.*
*The gravestone depicts the dead girl Hegeso, daughter of Proxenos (as the inscription at the top indicates). She is sitting on a domestic type of chair, her feet resting on a stool, choosing a necklace from the jewel case a maid is holding out to her. A religious interpretation has been suggested, in which the jewels symbolize the dead while the jewel case is the symbol of resurrection used in burial rites. The work can be attributed to the school of Callimachus and stood in the cemetery of Ceramicus, a district of Athens.*

*Page 58:* Female Head, *Classical art,* c. 420 B.C.
*Marble, height 10.6 in.*
*Athens, National Archeological Museum. A fragment of a lost statue, possibly depicting the goddess Hera. The wavy hair, parted in the middle and held in a band, is gathered into a chignon on the nape of the neck. From the west pediment of the Temple of Hera at Argos.*

*Right:* Female Head, *Classical art,* c. 460–450 B.C. Marble, height 10.3 in.
*Palermo, National Museum. Metope fragment from Temple E at Selinus, possibly representing a female deity.*

ΗΡΜΗΣ      ΕΥΔΙΚΗ      ΞΥΞΦΙΟ

152

*Left:* Hermes, Eurydice, and Orpheus,
*Classical art,* c. *420–410* B.C. *(contemporary copy).*
*Bas-relief, marble, height 46.9 in.*
*Naples, National Archeological Museum.*
*An ancient copy of a votive stele attributed to Callimachus
(or at any rate to Phidias' school) and depicting Eurydice
saying goodbye to her husband Orpheus (on the right),
with Hermes waiting to take her to the kingdom of the
dead.*

*Above:* Dioscuri, *Classical art,* c. *430–420* B.C.
*Parian marble, height 49.2 in.*
*This group and another similar one depict the Dioscuri
(the twins Castor and Polydeuces), each mounting a horse
while a Triton (a half-man, half-fish sea deity) holds the
animal's legs. The two groups stood as acroteria on a
temple near Locri. Legend has it that the Dioscuri came
out of the sea to lead the Locrians to victory against the
city of Croton.*

*Left:* Paeonius, Nike, *Classical art, 424* B.C.
*Marble, height 114.2 in.*
*Olympia, Museum.*
*This statue of Nike, the winged goddess who brought victory, was dedicated at Olympia by the inhabitants of Messene and Naupactus, who had helped the Athenians beat the Spartans in the battle of Sphacteria Island (425* B.C.*). It originally stood on a column 30 ft. high.*

*Page 59:* Anticythera Youth *(detail), Classical art, c. 340* B.C.
*Bronze, height 76.4 in.*
*Athens, National Archeological Museum.*
*The identity of the figure portrayed is uncertain. If the raised right hand held an apple, as has been suggested, it could be Heracles, picking the fruit in the garden of the Hesperides, or Paris handing the apple of victory to Aphrodite. Found in the sea off Anticythera.*

*Page 60:* Boxer's Head, *Classical art, c. 330* B.C. *Bronze, height 11 in.*
*Athens, National Archeological Museum.*
*A fragment of a lost statue, originally with inlaid eyes, erected as a votive offering in the Temple of Zeus at Olympia. It has been suggested that it portrays the athlete Satyros, winner of the 335* B.C. *Olympic Games, a statue of whom had been made by Silanion.*

*Right:* Thanatos and Alcestis *(?), by Artemision of Ephesus, Classical art, c. 350–340* B.C.
*Relief, marble, height 72.9 in.*
*London, British Museum.*
*A detail from a column base in the Temple of Artemis at Ephesus. The naked winged youth represents Thanatos, the god of death. On his right the male and female figures are probably Alcestis, the legendary heroine who agreed to die in place of her husband Admetus, and the god Hermes, who led the dead into Hades. The work has been attributed both to Scopas and to a sculptor of the Praxiteles school.*

*Left*: Aphrodite of Capua *(detail)*,
*Classical art, second half of the 4th century* B.C. *( Roman copy)*.
*Marble, height 82.7 in.*
*Naples, National Archeological Museum.*
*The original, traditionally attributed to Scopas, has now been ascribed to Lysippus and his school. The copy was made at the time of the Emperor Hadrian (* A.D. *117–138) to decorate the portico of the Capua amphitheater, where it was found at the beginning of the 18th century.*

*Above: Bryaxis,* Victorious Rider, *Classical art,*
c. *350* B.C. *Bas-relief, marble,*
*height 12.6 in., length of base 29.2 in.*
*Athens, National Archeological Museum.*
*One of three similar reliefs forming the sides of a statue base. It depicts a man on horseback advancing towards a tripod (a three-footed brazier). The work must therefore be a votive statue on the occasion of a horse-racing victory.*

157

Left: Demeter, *Classical art,*
*c. 340–330 B.C.*
*Parian marble,*
*height 60.3 in.*
*London, British Museum.*
*The goddess, completely enveloped in a*
*cloak, her head covered, is sitting on a*
*chair. The work, traditionally*
*attributed to Scopas, is now ascribed to*
*Leochares. From the sacred enclosure*
*of Demeter and Persephone at Cnidus*
*in Asia Minor.*

*Right: Praxiteles,* Head of Aphrodite
of Cnidus,
*Classical art, c. 360 B.C. (Roman*
*copy).*
*Marble, height 13.8 in.*
*Paris, Louvre.*
*A copy from the Hellenistic period*
*(beginning of the 3rd century B.C.) of an*
*original by Praxiteles. Known also as*
*the* Kaufmann Head, *after the*
*collector who owned it. The goddess*
*was depicted completely naked,*
*covering her pubes with her right hand,*
*her hair pulled into a chignon on the*
*nape of her neck. From her left hand a*
*cloak fell over an amphora, which,*
*according to iconographic tradition*
*common in Cnidus, was the symbol for*
*a ritual bath. Ancient commentators*
*regarded it as the sculptor's*
*masterpiece and gave the courtesan*
*Phryne as the statue's model.*

*Left: Timotheus,* Epione, *from the Temple*
*of Asclepius at Epidaurus, Classical art,*
*c. 385–375* B.C. *Marble, height 33.6 in.*
*Athens, National Archeological Museum.*
*This mutilated statue formed the central acroterium (a figure standing on the apex of a pediment) on the west side of the sanctuary of Asclepius, the god of medicine, at Epidaurus. It depicts Asclepius' wife Epione, who dispensed medicines, holding a cockerel (a symbol of life and sacred to Asclepius) in her right hand. The attribution to Timotheus is based on temple inscriptions, which also specify the sums paid to the various artists who worked there.*

*Page 61:* Eubuleus, *Classical art,*
*c. 340* B.C. *Marble, height 18.5 in.*
*Athens, National Archeological Museum.*
*This fragmentary bust portrays the legendary swineherd who, after the abduction of Persephone by Hades, was knocked into an abyss by the god's chariot. At Eleusis, where the myth of Persephone was worshiped in connection with nature's rebirth in the spring, Eubuleus was regarded as a local deity in charge of fertility. The work has been attributed both to Praxiteles and to an unknown sculptor of his school. From Eleusis.*

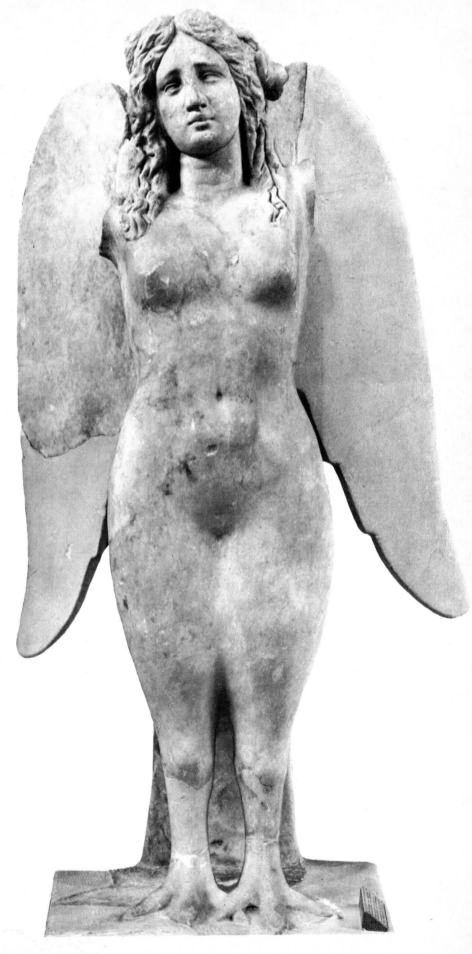

*Right:* Siren, *Hellenistic art, second half of the 4th century* B.C. *Marble, height 46 in. Athens, National Archeological Museum.*
*The siren was a creature with the body of a fish and the face of a woman. Similar to harpies or vampires, sirens had popularly been regarded as spirits of death since prehistoric times, particularly in Asia Minor. Sirens of the Hellenistic period, who in addition had the torso of a woman, became funerary guardian spirits and were depicted on the top of cemetery steles, as is the case in this example.*

*Left: Praxiteles*, Hermes and Dionysius *(detail)*,
*Classical art*, c. *340–330* B.C.
*(Hellenistic copy)*.
*Marble with traces of colour,
height 90.6 in.
Olympia, Museum.
The work depicts an episode from the
legend of Dionysius, the god of wine
and nature, who as a child was
entrusted to Hermes by his father Zeus.
According to Pausanias, the Temple of
Hera at Olympia contained work by
Praxiteles. When this group was found
in 1877 among the temple columns, it
was thought to be the original. It is now
regarded as a copy from the Hellenistic
period, possibly the work of another
Praxiteles, who lived in the 2nd century*
B.C. *and was a descendant of the earlier
sculptor.*

*Right: Lysippus*, Agias *(detail)*,
*Classical art*, c. *338–334* B.C.
*(contemporary copy)*.
*Marble, height 77.6 in.
Delphi, Museum.
The work depicts the famous Agias,
who in 408* B.C. *won many athletic
victories. The bronze original by
Lysippus formed part of a group of nine
statues that were dedicated at
Pharsalus by Daochus (a prince of
Thessaly who rose to power in 338* B.C.*)
and portrayed the sovereign and
his sons among victorious athletes. This
copy, probably from Lysippus'
workshop, formed part of a marble
replica of the group that Daochus
erected in the sanctuary of Apollo at
Delphi during the same period.*

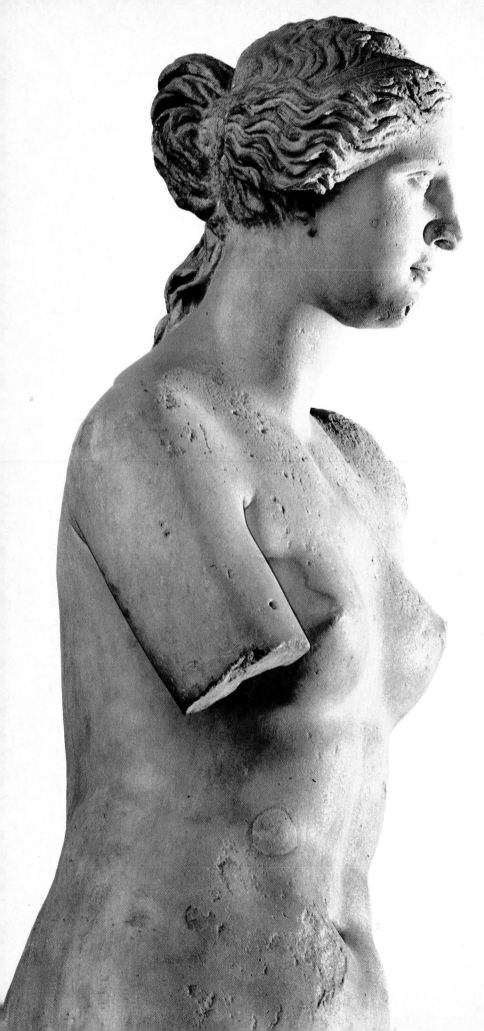

*Left:* Venus de Milo *(detail),
2nd–1st century* B.C. *(Hellenistic
copy).
Marble, height 79.6 in.
Paris, Louvre.
This Hellenistic copy (dating from the
end of the 2nd century* B.C. *or the
beginning of the 1st century) was
modelled on the same original as the
Aphrodite of Capua (see caption on
p. 157). A peasant from Milo in Italy
found fragments of it in his field in
1820.*

*Page 165, left:* Aphrodite of Sinuessa,
*Classical art, second half of the 4th
century* B.C.
*(Hellenistic copy).
Marble, height 70.9 in.
Naples, National Archeological
Museum.
Found by peasants at the beginning of
this century in a field near Mondragone
(ancient Sinuessa) in Italy, the statue
is a copy from the Hellenistic period,
dating from the beginning of the 2nd
century* B.C. *It belongs to the
Anadoumenos Aphrodite series and
portrays the goddess wringing out her
hair after emerging from the sea.*

*Page 165, right:* Female Figure,
*Hellenistic art,
2nd century* B.C. *Painted terra cotta,
height 9.8 in.
Taranto, National Museum.
The statuette, probably a domestic
ornament, depicts a woman with hair
gathered into a chignon, wearing a red
chiton (pleated tunic) and a large white
cloak edged in blue.*

*Pages 166 and 167:* Gigantomachy
*(detail),
from the Pergamum altar. Hellenistic
art,
c. 180* B.C. *High relief,
Asiatic marble, height 90.6 in.
Berlin, Staatliche Museen.
The battle between the gods and the
giants attempting to climb Olympus is
portrayed in the east frieze of the
Pergamum altar plinth. The detail
illustrated here shows Zeus on the left
(headless, with a cloak over his back
and legs) and Heracles on the right
(back view) defeating Porphyrion
(kneeling) in battle.*

*Left : Doedalsas,* Crouching Aphrodite,
*Hellenistic art,* c. *250* B.C. *( Roman copy).*
*Marble, height 38.6 in.*
*Paris, Louvre.*
*The goddess was probably shown washing her hair. A Roman copy of a bronze original from Sainte-Colombe near Vienne.*

*Page 63 :* Young Man Reading a Papyrus,
*Hellenistic art. Terra cotta, height 5.5 in.*
*Taranto, National Museum.*
*The statuette, made for funerary or domestic use (as an ornament), was found at Tarentum (now Taranto), which in the Hellenistic period was the largest center in Magna Graecia producing this kind of artifact, similar to work made in more famous centers.*

*Right :* Callipygian Aphrodite *(detail),*
*Hellenistic art,* c. *50* B.C.
*Marble, height 59.9 in.*
*Naples, National Archeological Museum. A Roman copy found in the Domus Aurea, Nero's palace in Rome, depicting the goddess "of the beautiful buttocks" taking off her cloak before a bath. She is glancing back, looking at herself in the water. The statue probably stood in the middle of a fountain.*

169

*Left:* Pan and Daphnis, *Hellenistic art,*
*second half of the 2nd century* B.C.
*Marble, height 65 in.*
*Naples, National Archeological Museum.*
*A Roman copy of a very common Hellenistic subject, the work portrays the god Pan teaching the shepherd Daphnis to play the pipes.*

*Page 62:* Eros and Psyche *(detail),*
*Hellenistic art, 3rd–2nd century* B.C.
*Terra cotta, height 8 in.*
*London, British Museum.*
*This small, erotic group from the Hellenistic period was made as an ornament and portrays the god of love and his wife kissing. From Centuripe in Sicily.*

*Right:* Aphrodite and Pan, *Hellenistic art,*
*c. 100* B.C. *Marble, height 52 in.*
*Athens, National Archeological Museum.*
*The group, intended for decoration, portrays the naked goddess, her left hand covering her pubes, using her sandal to drive off the god Pan, who is trying to seduce her. At the top, the small, laughing figure of Eros is helping his mother by tugging at one of the god's horns. From Delos.*

*Left :* Nike of Samothrace, *Hellenistic art,*
c. *190* B.C. *Rhodes marble with traces of colour,*
*height 10.7 ft.*
*Paris, Louvre.*
*This statue of the goddess originally stood on the prow of a ship in the middle of a small artificial lake in the theater at Samothrace. It commemorated the city's naval victory over the Rhodes fleet. She is portrayed winged, with a pleated garment and cloak clinging to her body and billowing over her back in the wind. The work was found in fragments in 1863.*

*Page 64 :* Barberini Faun *(detail), Hellenistic art,*
c. *220–210* B.C. *(Roman copy).*
*Marble, height 84.7 in.*
*Munich, Glyptothek.*
*The work, an ancient copy of an original from Pergamum, portrays a sleeping satyr, which was a very common subject in the Hellenistic period. It was found near Castel Sant'Angelo in Rome at the beginning of the 17th century. The Barberini family who acquired it had the missing parts replaced (right leg, parts of the left leg and arm, rock and tree) by Gian Lorenzo Bernini.*

*Right :* Psyche, *Hellenistic art,*
*1st century* B.C. *(Roman copy).*
*Marble, height 34.2 in.*
*Naples, National Archeological Museum.*
*The work, which was found at the beginning of the 18th century in the amphitheater at Capua, where it stood in the colonnade, is a copy of a Hellenistic original dating from the reign of Hadrian (*A.D. *117–138). Named "Psyche" at the time it was found, because its chaste attitude seemed to suit Eros' child-bride, it is more likely that it portrays Aphrodite scolding either Eros or a cupid at her feet.*

173

*Above:* Man's Head, *Hellenistic art,* c. *100* B.C. *Bronze, inlaid eyes, height 12.8 in. Athens, National Archeological Museum. Fragment of a lost statue. The figure portrayed was probably an athlete. From the Delos palaestra.*

# NOTES

## The Pre-Hellenic World

### GEOGRAPHICAL AREA

The pre-Hellenic civilizations developed on the island of Crete, in the Cyclades, on the Greek mainland, and in areas with a mixed Greco–Asiatic civilization: Troy in Asia Minor (modern Turkey) and the islands of Rhodes and Cyprus. The main archeological center in Crete, in the extreme south of the Aegean, is Knossos, a few kilometers from modern Heraklion, which used to be its port. Other important centers are at Mallia, Gournia, Palaikastro, Phaistos, and Hagia Triada. The island is dominated by the Ida massif (the location of the Kamares cave).

On the eastern side of Greece the Cyclades (from *kuklos*, circle) form an archipelago strung around Delos; the other islands are Amorgos, Melos (the location of Phylakopi), Naxos, Paros, and Thera (modern Santorini).

On the mainland the civilization embraced the Peloponnesus with its large centers of Mycenae, Tiryns, and Argos (Argolide) in Sparta (Laconia) and Pylos (Messinia). In Attica, Boeotia (Thebes and Orchomenus), and Thessaly there was less cultural activity.

In Asia the important centers were Troy in northern Asia Minor (on the modern hill of Hissarlik), the island of Rhodes with its centers of Ialysus, Camirus, and Lindus; and Cyprus, opposite the coast of Syria, with its towns of Enkomi, Kalopida, Larnaca, Vunus, and Episkopi.

### CHRONOLOGY

In the last phase of the Stone Age, the Neolithic, man began to organize the exploitation of natural resources; and this meant that he must live in permanent settlements. The following epoch, called the Bronze Age because it was during this time that bronze began to be used, is usually divided into three major periods: Early Bronze, Middle Bronze, and Late Bronze. It has various names—according to which cultural area we are referring to: *Minoan* in Crete (from the legendary King Minos of Knossos), *Helladic* on the Greek mainland, *Cycladic* in the Cyclades, and *Cypriot* in Cyprus. The chronology of Troy is based on the successive strata of buildings that were found on the hill at Hissarlik. The formulation of dates in years is necessarily approximate.

### EARLY BRONZE AGE

*Early Minoan*, or prepalatial (*c.* 2700–2000 B.C.): Marble idols and the beginning of seal engraving. *Early Helladic* (*c.* 2700/2500–2000 B.C.): Strong links with the Aegean world. *Early Cycladic* (*c.* 2700/2500–2000 B.C.): The most flourishing of these civilizations. Trade and contacts with Troy and the whole Aegean. Marble idols.

*Troy I–V* (*c.* 3000–1990 B.C.). Rapid development of urban civilization. Use of metal spread into the entire Aegean. Anthropomorphic vessels and stone and terra-cotta idols.

### MIDDLE BRONZE AGE

*Middle Minoan* (*c.* 2000–1570 B.C.): Flowering of Cretan civilization during the Old Palace period. The palaces, Knossos, Phaistos, and Mallia, were

Cycladic Idol, c. *2500–2000* B.C.
*Marble. From a grave in Teke.*
*Heraklion, Museum.*

175

ALPS

LIGURIA

Massilia

CORSICA

ETRURIA

Tiber

Caere ● ● Veii
● Rome

LATIUM

Cumae ●

Silarus

Tarentum
Paestum ●

SARDINIA

TYRRHENIAN SEA

Sybaris ●
Croton ●

Selinus ●

SICILY

Carthage ●

Rhegium ●

Magara Hyblaea ●
Syracuse ●

MALTA

MEDITERRANEAN SEA

Leptis Magna ●

ADRIATIC SEA

CARPATHIANS

Dniester

Danube

Dnieper

Olbia ●

TAURIC
CHERSONESUS

BLACK SEA (EUXINE)

THRACE

Byzantium ●  ● BITHYNIA

MACEDONIA

THASOS

Mount
Olympus

AEGEAN SEA

LESBOS

Troy ●

Pergamum ●

PHRYGIA

CORCYRA

EPIRUS

THESSALY

Thermon ●

EUBOEA

Delphi ●      Thebes ●
Corinth ●  ● Athens

Mycenae ●

Olympia ●    ● Argos

Sparta ●

PELOPONNESUS

LACONIA

Smyrna ●

CHIOS

● Sardis

LYDIA

DELOS

PAROS

AEGINA

MELOS

SAMOS

● Miletus

CARIA

NAXOS

COS

LYCIA

RHODES

Knossos ●

CRETE

Cyrene ●

Naukratis ●

LYBIAN DESERT

EGYPT

destroyed in about 1800, possibly in an earthquake. Hieroglyphic writing. Kamares ware. Clay figurines and seal engraving. *Middle Helladic* (*c.* 2000–1570 B.C.): Invasions of Indo–Europeans (*c.* 2000–1600 B.C.), who brought general stagnation and impoverishment. *Middle Cycladic* (*c.* 2000–1570 B.C.): The growing influence of Crete deprives the period of all independence.

LATE BRONZE AGE

*Late Minoan* (1570–1150 B.C.): New Palace period and another flowering of Cretan civilization. Statuettes (snake goddesses, ivory *Acrobat*), vases in relief, seal engraving. Linear A and B script. *Late Helladic* or *Mycenaean* (*c.* 1570–1000 B.C.): The destruction brought by the invasions was stemmed, and in Attica and Boeotia there developed a civilization centered on Mycenae, at first (Early and Middle Mycenaean, 1570–1500 B.C.) with strong Cretan influences, later (1400–1150/1100) with complete independence after the destruction of Knossos and other palaces (1450). The Mycenaean civilization spread into Thessaly, Macedonia, and the Cyclades (*Late Cycladic*, 1570–1100), and colonies were founded on Rhodes and Cyprus. In the twelfth century began a period of invasions and the great Mycenaean centers were destroyed. Monuments: fortified palaces. Sculpture: statuettes and small groups, gold funerary masks. *Troy VI*: At the end of the twelfth century came the Mycenaean expedition described in Homer's *Iliad*, and Troy was destroyed in 1184 B.C.

## RELIGION

The Cretan religion was centered on a few figures that personified and controlled the basic forces of nature, and this is supported by both artistic and written evidence (Linear B tablets). According to one interpretation, the mother-goddess of fertility and the male god fertilizer were worshiped in three areas of the universe (celestial, terrestrial, and subterranean), and these had their corresponding places of worship: mountain summits, groves, and caves. In general, deities were portrayed as zoomorphic or anthropomorphic (the mistress of wild beasts, the snake goddess, the dove goddess, and the bull god). Nevertheless, they were also believed to dwell in trees, sacred stones, and pillars. In their capacity as mothers, female deities were considered to be primordial. The three domains had corresponding symbols (for example the double axe, the horns of consecration, and the solar disc) and animals that accompanied the various deities (birds for celestial deities, wild or domestic animals for terrestrial ones, snakes and scarabs for the gods of the underworld). The cults involved processions, sacred representations of natural events, and ecstatic music and dancing to help establish contact with the deity.

As far as Mycenaean religion is concerned, there are major discrepancies between artistic and written records (Linear B tablets). The first contain evidence (preponderance of female idols, absence of temples) indicating that, like the Cretans, the Mycenaeans also worshiped a goddess. But the tablets, which were recently deciphered, contain references as early as the second millennium to Zeus, Hera, Poseidon, Athena, Hermes, Artemis, Ares, and Dionysius and so provide archeological evidence for Homer's references to Greek religion of the Mycenaean period. However, we have no information about whether these deities already had an anthropomorphic appearance. The

great Homeric myths of Heracles, Oedipus, and Minos have not been substantiated by documentary evidence.

## ICONOGRAPHY

A survey of pre-Hellenic sculpture from the iconographic point of view shows that basically human and animal figures were free-standing, while everyday subjects (including religious ceremonies) were shown in relief.

Typical of the Neolithic period are steatopygous statuettes (female figures with considerably enlarged hips, buttocks, and breasts), which were probably connected with the cult and portrayed the great mother-goddess. They have been found in large numbers in Thessaly, particularly at Sesklo and Dimini (near modern Volo) and in the Aegean areas of Asia Minor (pp. 80, 81).

Numerous Bronze Age idols have been found in the Cyclades. They are almost all female, although there are also some male figures, and they are generally upright, with arms crossed under the chest. There have been many theories about their meaning. It has been suggested that they represent odalisques, soul bearers, ecstatic heroes or nymphs, guardians of the dead, nursing mothers, magical talismans, the great mother-goddess, sea goddesses, and even toys. The Cyclades also produced interesting sculptures that look as if they were made of stones worn smooth by the sea. In a later period, standing flute players (p. 80) and seated lyre players (p. 34) were made. Vessels were often zoomorphic or anthropomorphic (shaped like a Syrian bear or a bull, p. 35). In Crete small-scale sculpture in the round continued to portray human and animal figures representing deities (snake goddesses, p. 85), votive offerings (cow suckling a calf), symbols (horns of consecration), or ornamental items such as a dog stretching itself (the figure was attached to the lid of a vessel).

177

Seals were carved with scenes connected with agriculture, religion, festivals, work, and sport (a potter at work, a fisherman with his fish, rows of animals, a man playing chess under a tree, women dancing wildly in a field of lilies in the presence of a goddess descending from heaven). The relief vases of Hagia Triada depict boxing and bullfighting, and there is also a scene showing a prince, with a scepter in his outstretched hand, giving orders to an officer of the guard who is standing at the head of a group of men armed with large shields. On the *Harvester Vase* is a procession of peasants holding pitchforks and poles. They are following a leading musician and singing at the tops of their voices. Apart from free-standing figurines similar to those that were made in Crete (the group portraying two goddesses with a child for example), the Mycenaean custom of putting embossed gold funerary masks over the faces of the dead has given us a series of "portraits" of Mycenaean kings (p. 38). The most famous relief vases are those made in Vaphio. They portray wild bulls being lassoed, before being broken and yoked (pp. 86, 87). And there is also the famous *Lion Gate*, whose enormous animals (10 feet high), the first example of monumental sculpture in Greece, were there to protect the palace (pp. 36–37).

## METHODS

The materials most commonly used in the pre-Hellenic period were terra cotta, marble, and bronze (an alloy of copper and tin), as well as ivory.

The oldest method of working terra cotta, which was already in use during the Cycladic civilization, consisted of making a piece of sculpture by winding a clay sausage onto a lathe or putting clay rings one on top of another and then joining them together. These systems were probably based on those used in making pottery. The technique of hollow ware, used in conjunction with the practice of adding fired clay and sand to the clay mixture, resulted in a more homogenous firing than that obtained by the traditional method of making solid ware. Modelling was done with the aid of a small spatula, which was sharpened at one end and straight at the other. But in general the hands were used. Colour was always applied with a brush, usually before the work was fired.

The earliest marble sculptures, some of the Cycladic idols for example, were produced by cutting sections of marble from a block with the aid of hammers and chisels, and then modelling them by abrasion using sand and emery.

The most primitive method of working bronze consisted of hammering out sheets of bronze, then nailing them onto a wooden core. The technique of solid *cire-perdue* (lost-wax) casting came later and was used to make small statuettes. The procedure consisted of first making a beeswax model of the object and then covering it with clay and sand. Entry and exit holes were made, and the mold was put into a kiln. When the wax melted it left an empty space into which molten bronze was poured.

## PURPOSE

Cycladic idols have been found in graves as well as in private dwellings. This means that they were not intended just for the cult of the dead. Nevertheless, our knowledge of their use is still quite incomplete. Cretan and Mycenaean sculpture, on the other hand, was generally connected with a cult, as indicated by the sites where finds have been made. Clay models of weasels and porcupines, probably linked to agricultural rites, have been found in the sanctuary of Juktas in Crete. Areas of the sanctuary rooms or even special shelves were reserved for statuettes of snake goddesses, goddesses of the

*Above:* Female Dancers, *pottery, Cretan art, 1450–1400* B.C. *Heraklion, Museum.*

*Top:* Two Goddesses with a Child, *Mycenaean art, 15th century* B.C. *Ivory. Athens, National Archeological Museum.*

hearth, animals, symbols and votary figures. They were either cult objects or the private offerings of the faithful.

## ARTISTS

We know nothing about individual Cretan and Mycenaean artists, but archeology has given us some information about their methods of working, their workshops, and their place in society.

There is no doubt that Cretan women had a very important place in all areas of social activity and this was equally true in art. Indeed, some scholars maintain that art was their prerogative. In general, sculptors worked in special rooms adjacent to palaces (at Gournia independent workshops have been found as well). The best artists were summoned to Knossos and housed in the royal palace, where workshops were put at their disposal. Inside the palace of Knossos was a small factory manufacturing jars and pitchers for the oil trade, and next to it were workshops producing luxury goods (engraved gems, statuettes, and various ornaments) bearing the royal seal.

On the Greek mainland, however, craftsmen (called *teti*) were independent and supplied the technical skills individual families and their slaves did not have. The profession was hereditary and artists were skilled in all aspects of working with a given type of material. The smith, for example, was able to work in bronze, iron, and gold, and to make weapons, pots, and jewelry. He was also the only one to have his own workshop; others worked wherever there was money to be earned. Yet artists were regarded as craftsmen, their individual skills making some more sought after than others.

# GREECE

## GEOGRAPHICAL AREA

Greek civilization developed in Greece (the Balkan peninsula) and on the coast of Asia Minor and its offshore islands. The area widened from the eighth to the sixth century with Greek colonial expansion towards the west into the Mediterranean and towards the northeast into the Black Sea. In southern Italy and Sicily the Greeks founded a network of colonies that would later be called Magna Graecia. On the mainland were Rhegium, Tarentum, Sybaris, Croton and other cities; in Sicily, Syracuse, Agrigentum, Megara Hyblaea, and Selinus. The Greek colonists thrust as far as Massilia (modern Marseilles) in southern France, the Iberian coast, Naukratis in Egypt, and Cyrene in Libya. A complex network of colonies was also founded on the northern coast of the Aegean, on the Sea of Marmara, and along the entire coastline of the Black Sea. The geography of the Greek world changed once again with Alexander the Great, who, during his expedition against the Persians, conquered the entire coastal area and Persia itself before pushing on as far as India. The new capitals of the states that were founded after Alexander's death were Alexandria in Egypt, Rhodes and Pergamum (modern Bergama) in Asia Minor, and Antioch in Syria.

## CHRONOLOGY

Greek civilization started to develop at the beginning of the Iron Age, and Greek art can be divided into four main periods.
FORMATIVE PERIOD (*c.* 1000–620 B.C.): Invasions of tribes from common Greek stock but speaking different dialects: Ionic, which became established in Attica; Aeolic in Thessaly, Corinth, and

*Above:* Temple of Poseidon *at Paestum,* c. *480–450* B.C.
*Top:* Assembled Gods, *frieze on the Temple of Athena Nike, end of the 5th century* B.C. *Athens, Acropolis.*

179

Arcadia; and Doric in the Peloponnesus. Colonies were later founded on the coasts of Asia Minor (eastern Greece, in its wider sense called Ionia), with the Ionians in the center, the Aeolians in the north, and the Dorians in the south. The Greeks felt a sense of nationhood as early as the eighth century, and this was demonstrated by, among other things, the writing of Homer's poems, the formation of the first sacred societies, and the beginning of colonial expansion.

ARCHAIC PERIOD (624–480 B.C.): By the end of the seventh century the polises, the cities that had been founded in the eighth century, had already developed into city-states. In 507, democracy was established in Athens. Towards the middle of the sixth century, the Persian empire began to threaten the cities of Ionia, and then Greece itself. Between 490 and 470, the Persian wars ended in Greek victory.

CLASSICAL PERIOD (480–330 B.C.): Pericles, the leader of Athens, pursued a policy of supremacy in Greece from 461 to 429. The Parthenon was built. From 431 to 404 Sparta fought against Athens in the Peloponnesian War. Athens was defeated, so losing all hope of supremacy. Civil wars followed and continued until Philip of Macedon conquered Greece in 338 and unified it against Persia. Philip was assassinated in 336, to be succeeded by Alexander.

HELLENISTIC PERIOD (330–31 B.C.): Leading an expedition against Persia, Alexander conquered all the Mediterranean coastal areas, annexed Persia, and extended his control as far as India. Greek culture, which in this late phase is called Hellenistic, spread into Asian and African territory. When Alexander died in 323, the empire broke up into several kingdoms, including Syria, Asia Minor, and Egypt. Greece remained under Macedonian control, but in 146 it became a Roman province. The Battle of Actium (31 B.C.) marked the Romans' definitive conquest of Egypt, the last of the independent Hellenistic kingdoms.

RELIGION AND MYTH

As we can see from Homer's poems, by the eighth century Greek religion already seems to be well formulated. Its basic feature was polytheism, which was connected to the Greeks' belief that the divine was present in every natural occurrence and in every human action. The gods were regarded as basically human (anthropomorphism) and this led to the creation of temples (where they dwelt) and effigies (called *agalma*, as distinct from *eikon*, which referred to a human image).

Olympus, the mountain on which the gods were believed to live, was ruled by a group of major deities, including Zeus, the god of heaven, who was supreme; Apollo, the god of the sun and the arts; Athena, the goddess of the sciences and war; and Aphrodite, the goddess of love. This subdivision of functions, which was also the result of the streamlining carried out by Greek mythographers, took no account of the strong local character of cults, where the patron deity of a city answered the needs of the local population.

Heracles was perhaps the most famous and the most represented of all legendary heroes. He was the son of Zeus and Alcmene and had to carry out twelve labours as a punishment for murdering his sons. He also fought the centaurs (Centauromachy), monstrous creatures who were half horse, half man. Other famous myths that were often portrayed were the Amazonomachy, the Greeks' battle against the Amazons, a tribe of warrior-women who did not admit males into their society (fought mainly by Heracles, Theseus, and Achilles); and the Gigantomachy, the battle between the gods and giants, the sons of the Gaea (the earth).

In Homer's poems the various acts connected with the cult—prayer, offering, and sacrifice—had also been codified. In addition the poems contained descriptions of public festivals, games,

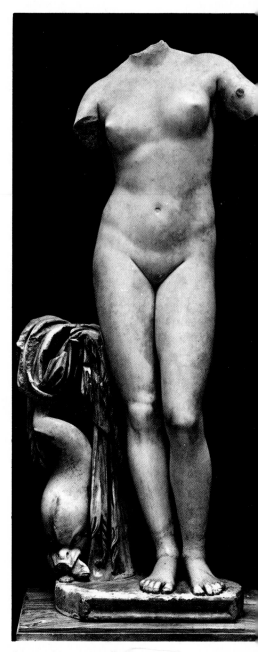

Cyrene Venus, *Hellenistic art, 2nd century* B.C. *Rome, National Museum of the Terme.*

and oracle consultations (Delphi was the most famous sanctuary for these). The Panathenaic and Dionysian festivals were two of the more famous ones. The important games included the Olympic, Isthmian, Nemean, and Pythian games. The cults relating to the Eleusinian Mysteries and Orphism, which both required initiation ceremonies, dealt with the question of life after death.

## ICONOGRAPHY

Compared with the Mycenaean period, basically only one subject was added to the Greek iconographic repertoire, and this was the portrayal of myth. Typical of the Archaic period were large *kouroi* and *korai* statues (the generic names indicate male and female figures of young men and women who were portrayed in motion or standing). The *kouros* was almost always a statue of a victorious athlete dedicated to a deity as a mark of gratitude.

Scenes from the myths began to appear towards the middle of the eighth century. The most portrayed were episodes showing the labours of Heracles. The pediment of the ancient Hekatompedon on the Acropolis depicts his fight with Triton, the half-man, half-fish monster of the sea; the metopes of Temple C at Selinus show Heracles fighting against the Cercopes; while on the east pediment of the Siphnian Treasury at Delphi, Apollo and Heracles are shown fighting for the tripod.

Nevertheless, scenes from the Greeks' daily life continued to be portrayed. There is an Athenian statue base with scenes from a ball game and a scene with a dog and cat (pp. 112–13); and elsewhere a kind of hockey game is illustrated.

Apart from figures of gods and athletes, such as Myron's *Discobolus*, myth remained the main subject of architectural sculpture in the Classical period. However, feelings were beginning to emerge, not only in the statue's pose but in its facial expression as well. This led to the emergence of portraiture, such as the *Head of Themistocles* (a Roman copy found at Ostia).

The Parthenon reliefs give us a fairly complete picture of the myths Greek artists portrayed most often. The metopes on its four sides depict, respectively, episodes from the Centauromachy (pp. 143–44), the Gigantomachy, the Amazonomachy, and the fall of Troy (practically all of this last side has been lost). On the internal frieze of the colonnade there are scenes from the Panathenaic festivities (pp. 140–42); while the pediment illustrates the birth of Athena (pp. 134–39) and her contest with Poseidon for control of the city.

In the Hellenistic period sculptors began to be more graphic, increasing their subject matter to include portrayals of childhood, old age, ethnic groups, and drunkenness.

The portrait became part of Greek iconography for similar reasons. The period produced a great many portraits of Alexander, but there was also a portrait of Menander (now in the Boston Museum) and one of Epicurus (now in the Metropolitan Museum of New York). Naturally this process also led to the emergence of historical themes, for example the battle between the Romans and Macedonians illustrated on a statue base found at Delphi (second century B.C.).

## METHODS

Like their pre-Hellenic counterparts, Greek sculptors generally used terra cotta, marble, and bronze. The chryselephantine technique, which combined gold and ivory, was an innovation dating from the Archaic period.

Methods of making articles from clay did not undergo any drastic changes. The only difference was that when large statuary began to be made, protruding members and other details (such as hair, beard, parts of the clothing, and jewelry), which were sometimes made from different materials, were added after the body was finished. From the seventh century, molds for mass production were made from a prototype by covering it with a clay jacket and then firing it in a kiln. The molds were then carefully stored, as indicated by finds in Corinthian workshops (from the seventh to the third centuries B.C.).

For large-scale marble statuary the usual practice was to produce a rough outline of the blocks while they were still *in situ* so as to simplify transport from the quarry. Chisels were used to carve the marble, the protruding parts of the anatomy generally being made separately and joined to the body later—with cement if they were small or with wedge-shaped metal pins. As in terra cotta, the practice of adding details made from different materials was very common. Coloured stone, ivory, or glass paste was used for eyes; metal for curls, eyelashes, jewelry, spears, swords, reins, and bridles. Various methods, all of them mechanical, were used to remove the marble's surface opacity, ranging from gentle rubbing with coarse marble blocks to the use of abrasive powders.

As far as bronze was concerned, the Greeks made a fundamental technical breakthrough around the seventh century. The technique of hollow casting had been imported from Egypt, and this enabled them to make large statues. Compared with the solid casting method, the new technique consisted of making a wax model over a clay core and covering it with clay. After firing, the molten bronze was poured into the cavity left by the wax. These statues were not painted, but left their natural golden-yellow colour. Bronze was the favourite material in the Classical period, and it was particularly popular with Myron and Polyclitus.

When bronze alloy was being made the copper and tin were mixed in various proportions according to the effect the artist wanted to achieve. Other metals, such as gold and silver, were often added to the compound to give the finished article a particular quality. The shortage of these materials in later periods was a contributing factor in the almost total disappearance of such statues. Among the very few that have luckily survived are the *Piombino Apollo* (p. 49), the *Delphi Charioteer* (pp. 53, 119), and the *Cape Artemisium Poseidon* (p. 119).

The chryselephantine technique was an amalgam, combining the use of embossed gold and engraved ivory. To make a large statue in this way the artist had first of all to build a complex wooden armature, and then engrave and carve it before applying thin strips of heated ivory to areas corresponding to the flesh. Gold plate was used for the head, clothes, and other details. In the Classical period this technique was used only for statues of deities, such as Phidias' famous duo: the *Zeus* for the Temple of Olympia and the *Athena Parthenos* for the Parthenon, both of which have been lost.

## PURPOSE

Like the sculpture of Crete and Mycenae, Greek sculpture was almost entirely connected with the requirements of religion. A statue of a deity was placed in the naos (the largest room in a Greek temple as well as the most important, the place where the deity dwelt). In the area around the temple stood the votive statues that had been given by the faithful. The statues were both private (for favours received) and public (for victory in war, a win in a competition, or a treaty between two cities). These offerings sometimes stood inside the temple as well. The Temple of Apollo at Delphi, for example, contained among other things a bronze

statue of Homer; inscribed on the base was the oracle's reply to the poet's anxious request to know from which Greek city he came. Sculptures commissioned by private individuals for grave monuments (steles, carved slabs, free-standing statues, or relief vases) were erected outdoors in both private burial grounds and public cemeteries, such as the Ceramicus in Athens.

In about the fifth century, commemorative statues of important people began to be erected in public squares, for example, the *Harmodius and Aristogiton* group erected on the market square of Athens in honour of the two heroes who had killed the tyrant Hipparchus. This trend grew more marked in the Hellenistic period, when statues began to appear in private houses as well.

Only certain parts of a temple carried relief decoration. These were the pediment, which was a triangular area on the temple façade bound by the sloping sides of the roof (a pediment might also contain statues) and the frieze, a part of the trabeation above the architrave, which was composed of either figural metopes alternating with decorative Doric triglyphs or a continuous Ionic fascia. Friezes were also used to decorate the sides of altars. Treasuries (buildings housing public gifts) were decorated with reliefs in the same manner as temples.

The function of small-scale sculpture in the round on tripods, handles, vessels, mirrors, and other items was purely decorative. Statuettes were made as votive offerings and placed in sanctuaries or on graves. Notable examples are the famous terra-cotta statuettes found in the Tanagra necropolis in Boeotia. Hellenistic workshops made decorative articles.

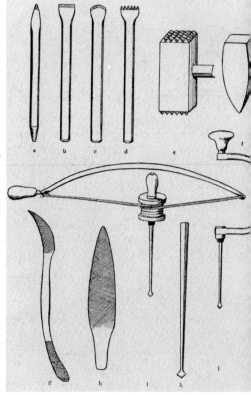

Sculptor's tools:
a) *point or punch*,
b–c–d) *chisels*,
e–f) *hammers, boucharde and pointed*,
g–h) *rasps*,
i) *running drill*,
k) *drill*,
l) *auger*.

## ARTISTS

The concept of the artist-craftsman, which had been current in the Bronze Age, continued into the Greek period. And the fact that neither architecture nor sculpture figured among the nine Muses and that artists were never included among portraits of famous men are indicative of this. Artists continued to be regarded as manual workers who did not merit the same respect as people who worked with their brains. Nevertheless, from the seventh century the name of the artist began to appear on the statue base next to the name of the donor and the deity being portrayed. The most famous whose signatures have been found include Polyclitus, Praxiteles, Cephisodotus, Kresilas, and Lysippus. Individual personalities were therefore beginning to emerge. This change can also be seen in the appearance of myths about legendary artists, such as Daedalus, the archetypal sculptor, and Epeus, who had built the Trojan Horse.

The reputation of some sculptors spread beyond their hometowns, and they received commissions from other places. (We have evidence of this from as early as the seventh century, when the sculptor Bathycles of Magnesia was asked to go and work in Sparta.) Sculptors also visited sanctuaries throughout the Hellenic world in search of commissions, and some held permanent exhibitions in Delphi and Olympia.

Ambitious works such as the sculptures for the Parthenon were obviously produced by teams. Hundreds of labourers, marble workers, painters, and goldsmiths worked for some fifteen years under Phidias' direction to complete this project.

The work artists of the Archaic and Classical periods were commissioned to do was concerned primarily with religion; public demand therefore had a collective character. Under Alexander the Great, and later under the Diadochi who had divided the empire among themselves, rulers began to want more propaganda for their achievements, while rich, private individuals wanted works to decorate their houses and so enhance their standing. Artists were therefore also chosen on account of their personal prestige. Nevertheless the concept of the artist-craftsman did not change. Even Plato called them *demiourgoi* ("craftsmen" or, more accurately, "public servants"). This attitude would remain unchanged in the Roman period.

## COPIES

The Classical and Hellenistic Greek sculpture that we have been familiar with for centuries had a strange fate. It is known almost entirely through copies dating from a later period. Exceptions are rare. Phidias' work (middle of the fifth century B.C.) survives in the metopes, friezes, and statues of the Parthenon (apart from conceiving the whole plan, he may possibly have actually helped to make the works). As for Scopas, who was active in the fourth century B.C., there are several fragmentary works by him, certainly original (from the Temple of Athena Alea at Tegea). However Scopas' most famous works (the *Menander* and the *Meleager*) have also survived in Roman copies. The same is true of Phidias, and there are copies of his *Athena Lemnia*, mainly the torso (in the Albertina Museum in Dresden) and the head (in the Civic Museum in Bologna). The chryselephantine *Zeus* of Olympia (also by Phidias), which was regarded as one of the seven wonders of the world, is known only through reproductions on gems and coins. There are a great many copies of Myron's *Discobolus* (Myron was active between 470 and 440), including one in the National Museum in Rome. Polyclitus' *Doryphorus* (second half of the fifth century) has survived in

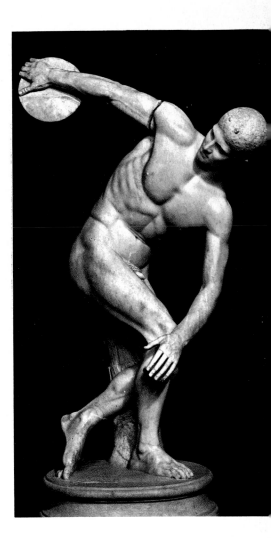

*Myron,* Discobolus, c. *470–440* B.C. *(Lancellotti copy). Rome, National Museum of the Terme (see p. 20).*

copies in the Museum of Naples and the Uffizi in Florence. Lysippus' *Apoxyomenus* (*c.* 370 B.C.) has survived in a marble copy from the Roman period. Praxiteles' *Hermes and Dionysius* is probably a second-century copy.

Johann Winckelmann, the scholar responsible for the emergence of modern classical archeology, also thought that the statues he found in Rome at the end of the eighteenth century were Greek originals. The credit for solving the problem of copies belongs mainly to the "philological" school of the nineteenth century. Karl Friedrichs, for example, in order to identify a copy in the Museum of Naples as the *Doryphorus*, used literary information from Pliny and Quintilian as well as his belief that the original must have been in bronze (since the hair was portrayed so accurately). Analyzing the stylistic features of the work, he eventually attributed it definitely to Polyclitus.

The practice of making copies goes back to ancient times. As early as the fourth century B.C., the Greeks regarded the works of the previous century as classical and therefore to be copied. In the Roman period we have definite evidence that Cicero and Lucullus were keen collectors of Classical statues and paintings. The Romans were in fact the greatest collectors of copies and originals (replicas were left in the place of originals when these were removed). Workshops sprang up to satisfy the growing demand, and in Ephesus, Smyrna, Paros, Thasos, Pergamum, and Magna Graecia genuine schools developed. But the Greek workshops remained the best, especially those in Athens.

Originals were often chosen not according to how good they were, but according to where the copies were to go. So athletes were chosen for gymnasiums, sea deities for baths, and austere statues of religious figures for meeting places. Marble, which was less expensive, was generally also used to copy bronze originals, and there is only one known case of direct casting from an older bronze (a torso in the Archeological Museum in Florence). The use of marble meant employing supports and props to carry transversal parts (this had not been necessary for the bronze originals). And since some details of finer workmanship were difficult to copy in marble (locks of hair or the line of the eyelids, for example) the traditional practice of inserting eyes of coloured stones and using various materials to make other details came back into fashion. Replicas were often made just of the head, or the work was done on a smaller scale, in clay for example. Well-made copies were greatly valued, and many of them bore the artist's signature as if they were actually original works. Apart from Roman copies, some of which are even now difficult to tell from the originals, various Renaissance imitations have survived. And in the second half of the eighteenth century and the beginning of the nineteenth century, neoclassical artists went back to copying Greek statues, following in the footsteps of the ancient copyists in their belief that the statues of the Classical and Hellenistic periods were masterpieces.

## DESTRUCTION AND REDISCOVERY

Centuries of civil and economic instability, barbarian invasions, and bloodshed do not in themselves explain the methodical destruction of Classical art. The new Christian culture's hatred of the "pagans" was even officially sanctioned by governments. Theodosius II, Emperor of the Eastern Empire, issued a decree in A.D. 426 ordering the destruction of all temples. Many, particularly in Rome, were turned into Christian churches.

But the most systematic sacking took place in the late Middle Ages when new buildings were made using materials taken from pagan temples. The little that was left untouched was allowed to fall into ruin. The admiration felt by important contemporary writers is therefore all the more interesting. Dante, for example, spoke highly of Polyclitus, even though his knowledge of his work came second-hand, via scholarly Roman sources.

The destruction of the Mausoleum at Halicarnassus by the Knights of Saint John (1403), the devastation of the Colosseum (1460) by Pius II, and the conversion of the Parthenon into a mosque by the Turks are just three of the many examples of destruction at the hands of both Christians and Moslems. In 1687 the Venetians bombarded the Athens Acropolis, and there are countless examples of the damage that was done in Rome during the course of a thousand years (works from Classical Greece, mostly sculpture, had been pouring into Rome since the first century A.D.).

But parallel to this, particularly from the fifteenth century onwards, there were increasingly frequent papal and royal edicts and decrees for the preservation of the work that had survived. In 1471, Sixtus IV started the municipal Capitoline collection of ancient sculptures. This was quickly copied by other churchmen, emperors, and nobles, and both public and private collections were founded. This trend was given great impetus by the writings of humanists like Flavio Biondo and Poggio Bracciolini and by the architect Leon Battista Alberti, who supported the theoretical work with a great deal of restoration and reconstruction in this period. After the first discoveries (the finding of the *Laocoön* in Rome dates from 1506), further investigation led to new finds, culminating in the discovery of Pompeii and Herculaneum in the eighteenth century.

In the following decades the monumental works of Johann Winckelmann were published, and this led to increased interest in the critical and systematic study of antiquity. Myron's *Discobolus* was identified in 1783, Polyclitus' *Doryphorus* was discovered in 1797, and the *Venus de Milo* was discovered in 1820.

The nineteenth century was dominated by the romantic figure of Heinrich Schliemann. He was passionately interested in the ancient civilizations described by Homer, and he eventually discovered Troy (1870) and the palace of Mycenae (1876). In 1900 Sir Arthur Evans began to excavate Knossos and Phaistos in Crete.

Modern scientific archeology did not emerge until the nineteenth century. Before then scholars had been forced to rely mainly on literary sources to study the history of Classical works of art. Information was obtained from fragments of prose and poetry (Homer, Herodotus' *Histories*, and Thucydides' *History*), in which works of art and artists were mentioned. More detailed information and comment was found in specialized literature, but since this had been written in later periods it meant it was the product of a culture very different from the one that had produced the original works. For this reason such literature often had very little objective value.

The most valuable and complete ancient source is Pliny the Elder's *Naturalis Historia* (first century A.D.). It is a collection of facts about the natural world, but in discussing some of its aspects, such as stone, marble, metal, bronze, and various kinds of clay, Pliny also brought in sculpture and painting, to give a full account of all the information then available about the decorative arts. Another source was Pausanias' *Description of Greece* (second century A.D.), which is a kind of guide—in ten volumes—containing a great many facts about places and monuments.

*Above:* East Pediment of the Parthenon, *drawing by Carrey (1674), with some of the sculptures still* in situ.
*Top:* Erechtheum, *view by James Stuart (1750).*

185

## MUSEUMS

### ATHENS

*National Archeological Museum*, founded in 1881. Department of Cycladic and Mycenaean art (including Schliemann's finds from Mycenae). Very large collection of Greek sculpture.

*Acropolis Museum*, founded in 1863, enlarged in 1953. Collection of items found on the Acropolis, including a magnificent series of *korai*; a fragment of frieze from the Parthenon, depicting Apollo, Artemis, and Poseidon; and fragments of the Victories that decorated the parapet of the Temple of Athena Nike.

### BERLIN

*Staatliche Museen*, complex of state museums founded in 1826; from 1945 divided between the city's east and west sectors. The Dahlem Museums in West Berlin include the Pergamum Museum, which contains the altar that K. Humann found at Pergamum in 1878 and restored. In the same complex is the Graeco-Roman Museum (Antikensammlungen), which has a department of Greek sculpture.

### BOSTON

*Museum of Fine Arts*. Department of Greek sculpture established in 1872.

### HERAKLION (CRETE)

*Archaeological Museum*, founded in 1878 and rebuilt after the Second World War. The most important and complete museum of the Cretan civilization.

### LONDON

*British Museum*, founded in 1753. The department of Greek sculpture was started in 1805 and greatly enlarged in 1816 with sculpture from the Erechtheum and most of the Parthenon friezes, which had been removed to London by Lord Elgin, the British ambassador in Constantinople.

### MUNICH

*Antikensammlungen*. Department of Greek sculpture (friezes from the temple on Aegina).

### NAPLES

*National Archeological Museum*, formerly the Borbonico Museum, moved to its present building in 1822. Established in the second half of the 1700s with the Farnese collections, inherited by Charles II of Bourbon, and with finds from new excavations at Pompeii, Herculaneum, and Stabio, mostly Roman copies of Greek works (Polyclitus' *Doryphorus*, Praxiteles' *Eros*, the *Farnese Heracles*, *Farnese Bull*, and the *Dying Gaul*).

### NEW YORK

*Metropolitan Museum*, founded in 1872. Important department of Greek art.

### OXFORD

*Ashmolean Museum*, founded in 1863. Important department of Aegean art (Cycladic idols, finds from Sir Arthur Evans's excavations in Crete).

### PALERMO

*National Museum*, founded in 1814, in its present building from 1866. Department of Greek sculpture established with Bourbon donations and finds from Selinus, Imera, and Syracuse.

### PARIS

*Louvre*. Department of Greek sculpture opened in about 1820, when the ambassador at Constantinople, Rivière, sent Louis XIV the *Venus de Milo* as a gift. The department grew as a result of archeological expeditions during the reign of Napoleon III, 1848–1870 (one find was the *Nike of Samothrace*).

### ROME

*National Roman Museum* (or *Museum of the Terme*), founded in 1889. Collection of Greek sculpture (*Ludovisi Throne*, Myron's *Discobolus*).

*Capitoline Museums*. Department of Greek sculpture established with successive papal donations, starting with one made by Sixtus IV in 1471 (*Portrait of Homer*, *Capitoline Venus*, *Dying Gaul*).

*Vatican Museums*. Department of Greek sculpture (*Laocoön* group, *Belvedere Torso*, *Apollo Belvedere*).

### SYRACUSE

*Archaeological Museum*. Department of Greek sculpture, created in 1811 from a private collection and enlarged with finds from numerous later excavations.

186

# BIBLIOGRAPHY

Becatti, G. *La scultura greca. I, Dalle origini al V secolo. II, Il IV secolo.* Milan, 1961.

Bianchi Bandinelli, R. *Introduzione all'arte classica come storia dell'arte antica.* Bari, 1976.

Bieber, M. *The Sculpture of the Hellenistic Age.* New York, 1961.

Blegen, C. W., et al. *Troy. I, General Introduction, The First and Second Settlements,* Princeton, 1950; *II, The Third, Fourth and Fifth Settlements,* 1951. *III, The Sixth Settlement,* 1953.

Blümel, C. *Die archaisch-griechischen Skulpturen der Staatlichen Museen zu Berlin.* Berlin, 1963.

———. *Die klassisch-griechischen Skulpturen der Staatlichen Museen zu Berlin.* Berlin, 1966.

———. *Griechische Bildhauer an der Arbeit.* Berlin, 1941; English ed., 1969 (3rd ed.).

Bossert, H. Th. *Altkreta* (3rd ed.). Berlin, 1937.

Chamoux, F. *La civilisation grecque à l'époque archaïque et classique.* Paris, n.d.

Charbonneaux, J. *L'Art égéen.* Paris, 1929.

———. *Sculpture grecque archaïque.* Paris, 1939.

———. *Sculpture grecque classique* (2 vols.). Paris, 1943, 2 vols.

Charbonneaux, J., Martin, E., and Villard, F. *Grèce archaïque, Grèce classique, Grèce hellénistique.* Paris, 1968, 1969, 1970 (L'Univers des formes).

Childe, V. G. *The Dawn of European Civilization* (6th ed.). London, 1957.

Demargne, P. *La Crète dédalique.* Paris, 1947.

———. *Naissance de l'art grec.* Paris, 1964 (L'Univers des formes).

Devambez, P. *L'art au siècle de Périclès.* Lausanne, 1955.

Diepolder, H. *Die attischen Grabreliefs des 5. und 4. Jahrhunderts v. Ch.* Berlin, 1931.

Ducati, P. *L'arte classica.* Turin, 1956 (3d ed.).

Dussaud, R. *Les civilisations préhelléniques dans le bassin de la mer Egée.* Paris, 1910, 1914.

*Enciclopedia dell'arte antica, classica e orientale* (9 vols., including supplement and atlas). Rome: Istituto della Enciclopedia Italiana, Fondazione Treccani, 1958–1973.

Evans, A. *The Palace of Minos at Knossos* (4 vols. with indexes). London, 1921–1935.

———. *The Shaft Graves and Beehive Tombs of Mykenae.* London, 1929.

Glotz, G. *La civilisation égéenne.* Paris, 1923.

Helbig, W. *Führer durch die öffentliche Sammlungen klassischer Altertümer in Rom, I–II,* (new rev. ed.). Tübingen, 1963–1966.

Higgins, R. H. *Catalogue of the Terracottas in the Department of Greek and Roman Antiquities, British Museum, II–III.* London: British Museum, 1900–1904.

Homann-Wedeking, E. *Das archaische Griechenland.* Baden-Baden, 1966.

Hutchinson, R. W. *Prehistoric Crete.* Harmondsworth, 1962.

Johansen, K. F. *The Attic Gravereliefs of the Classical Period, an Essay on Interpretation.* Copenhagen, 1951.

Karouzou, S. *Musée Archéologique nationale. Collection des sculptures, Catalogue descriptif.* Athens, 1968.

Langlotz, E. *Die Kunst der Westgriechen in Sizilien und Unteritalien.* Munich, 1963.

Lippold, G. *Die Skulpturen des Vatikanischen Museums. (Deutsches Archäologisches Institut,* III, 1–2.) Berlin, 1936–1956.

Lullies, R. *Griechische Skulptur von den Anfängen bis zum Ausgang des Hellenismus* (2d ed.). Munich, 1960.

Mansuelli, G. A. *Galleria degli Uffizi. Le sculture.* Rome, 1958–1961.

Marinatos, Sp., and Hirmer, H. *Kreta und das mykenische Hellas.* Munich, 1959.

Matz, F. *Geschichte der griechischen Kunst. I, Die geometrische und die früharchaïsche Form.* Frankfurt a. M., 1950.

———. "Die Agaïs," in *Handbuch der Archäologie,* II, pp. 179–308. Munich, 1950.

———. *Kreta, Mykene, Troja.* Stuttgart, 1956.

———. *Kreta und frühes Griechenland.* Baden-Baden, 1962.

Mendel, G. *Catalogue des sculptures grecques, romaines et byzantines* (3 vols.). Constantinople, 1912–1914.

Mollard-Besques, S. *Catalogue raisonné des figurines et reliefs en terre cuite grecs et romains, II, Myrina* (2 vols.). (Musée du Louvre et Collections des Universités de France.) Paris, 1963.

Montelius, O. *La Grèce préclassique, I–II.* Stockholm, 1924–1928.

Mylonas, G. E. *Ancient Mycenae: The Capital City of Agamemnon.* Princeton, 1957.

Neugebauer, K. A. *Die Griechischen Bronzen der klassischen Zeit und des Hellenismus (Staatliche Museen zu Berlin, Katalog der statuarischen Bronzen, II).* Berlin, 1951.

Paribeni, E. *Museo Nazionale Romano. Sculture greche del V secolo. Originali e Repliche (Cataloghi dei Musei e Galleria d'Italia).* Rome, 1953.

Pendlebury, J. D. S. *The Archeology of Crete.* London, 1939.

Pernier, L., and Banti, L. *Guida agli scavi Italiani in Creta.* Rome, 1947.

Picard, Ch. *Manuel d'archéologie greque. La sculture: I, Période archaïque; II, Période classique; III, Période hellénistique.* Paris, 1935–1966.

Platon, N. *Creta.* Geneva, 1975.

Poulsen, F. *Catalogue of Ancient Sculpture in the Ny Carlsberg Glyptotek.* Copenhagen, 1951.

Pryce, F. N. *Catalogue of Sculpture in the Department of Greek and Roman Antiquities of the British Museum, I, Part I, Prehellenic and Early Greek.* London, 1928.

Richter, G. M. A. *Three Critical Periods in Greek Sculpture.* Oxford, 1951.

———. *Catalogue of Greek*

*Sculptures, Metropolitan Museum of Art.* Cambridge, Mass., 1954.

————. *A Handbook of Greek Art.* London, 1959.

————. *Kouroi, Archaic Greek Youths.* London, 1960.

————. *The Portraits of the Greeks* (3 vols.). London, 1965.

————. *Korai, Archaic Greek Maidens.* London, 1968.

Ridder, A. de. *Les Bronzes antiques du Louvre* (2 vols.). Paris, 1914–1915.

Schachermeyr, F. *Die ältesten Kulturen Griechenland.* Stuttgart, 1955.

Schede, M. *Griechische und römische Skulpturen des Antikenmuseums.* Berlin–Leipzig, 1928 (*Meisterwerke der turkischen Museen zu Kostantinopel, I*).

Schefold, K. *Griechische Kunst als religiöse Phänomen*, n.p., n.d.

————. *Klassisches Griechenland.* Baden-Baden, 1966.

Schliemann, H. *Trojanische Ältertümer.* Leipzig, 1874.

————. *Mykenae.* Leipzig, 1878.

————. *Orchomenos.* Leipzig, 1881.

————. *Ilios.* Leipzig, 1881.

————. *Troja.* Leipzig, 1884.

————. *Tiryns.* Leipzig, 1886.

Smith, A. H. *Catalogue of Sculpture in the Department of Greek and Roman Antiquities, British Museum, II, III.* London, 1900–1904.

Thompson, H. A. *The Athenian Agora, a Guide to the Excavations and Museum* (2d ed.). Princeton, N.J.: American School of Classical Studies at Athens, 1962.

Webster, T. B. L. *Hellenismus.* Baden-Baden, 1966.

Zervos, Ch. *L'Art de la Crète néolithique et minoënne.* Paris, 1956.

————. *L'art des Cyclades du début à la fin de l'age du Bronze.* Paris, 1957.

————. *Naissance de la civilisation en Grèce* (2 vols.). Paris, 1963.

# INDEX

# PHOTOGRAPHIC SOURCES

The abbreviations t, b, c, r, l refer to the position of the illustration on the page (top, bottom, center, right, left)

Aldo Ballo, Milan
63

British Museum, London
4, 134–135, 136–137, 138, 139, 140, 141, 143, 144, 145, 146t, 147b, 155, 158

Deutsches Archaeologisches Institut, Athens
88

Farabola-Alinari, Milan
99b

John Freeman, London
185b, c

Prof. Walter Hege, Weimar
13

M. Holford, London
47

Kodansha, Tokyo
46, 50, 54

Koppermann, Munich
64, 97, 122, 123, 125, 132, 133

© Librairie Gallimard, Paris (*Arte Egea*, di Pierre Demargne); Photo U.D.F.
175, 178t

Metropolitan Museum of Art, New York
93

Antonia Mulas, Milan
51, 55, 62

Museum of Fine Arts, Boston
90, 120

Nippon Keizai Shimbun, Tokyo
103

© Phaidon, London (*Greek sculptors at work*, by C. Blümel)
182

François René Roland, Paris
6, 21, 30, 33, 34, 35, 36, 38, 39, 40, 41, 42, 43, 44–45, 48, 49, 52, 53, 56, 57, 58, 59, 60, 61, 66, 70, 78, 80, 81, 82, 83, 84, 85, 86, 87, 89, 91, 92, 94, 95, 96, 98, 99a, 100, 101, 104–105, 105b, 106, 107, 108, 109, 110, 111, 112, 113, 114, 115, 116, 117, 118, 119, 121, 124, 126, 127, 128, 129, 130, 131, 142, 148, 149, 150, 151, 152, 153, 154, 156, 157, 159, 160, 161, 162, 163, 164, 165l, 168, 169, 170, 171, 172, 173, 174

Royal Institute of British Architects, London
185t

Soprintendenza Archeologica, Taranto

Staatliche Museen, Berlin
102l, 102r, 166–167

© Weidenfeld and Nicolson, London (*The Acropolis* by R.J. Hopper); photo by Werner Forman, London.
179t

Arnoldo Mondadori Archives, Milan
Milan
2, 29, 75, 179b